Up, Down, and All Around

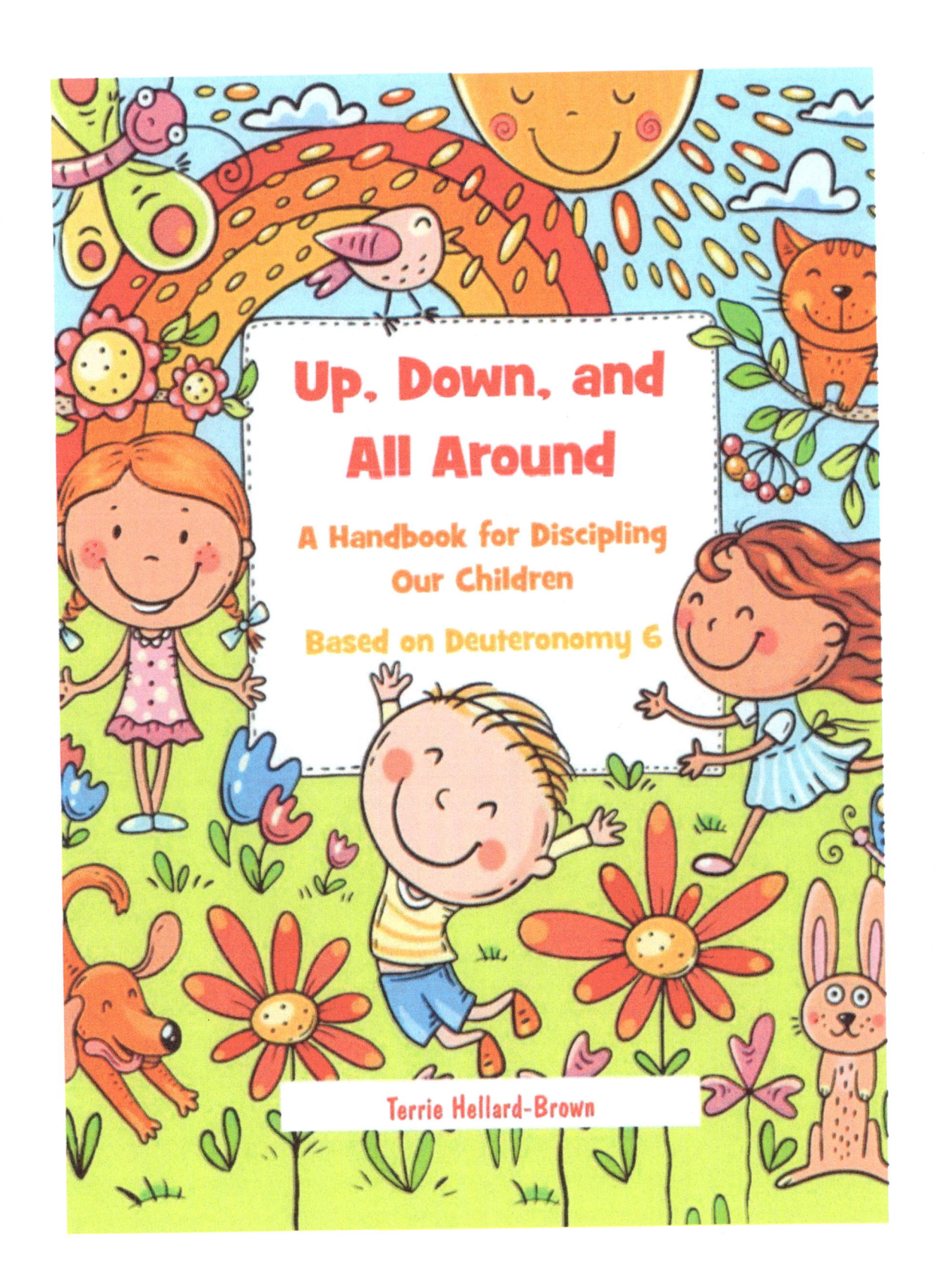

A Handbook for Discipling Our Children

Based on Deuteronomy 6

Terrie Hellard-Brown

*Dedicated to
Rachelle, Nathaniel, Annalyssa, and Ryan,
my most important calling of all*

**Do what God's teaching says:
don't just listen and do nothing.
When you only sit and listen,
you are fooling yourselves.
(James 1:22, ERV)**

Text copyright © 2024 by Terrie Hellard-Brown. All rights reserved.

Child Characters/Icons/Cover Art by Katerina Davidenko.

Copyright © 2024 by Hypurpley Press.

Editing by Dina Schlie Preuss.

No portion of this book may be reproduced, stored in an electronic retrieval system, or transmitted in any form or by any means—electronic, mechanical, photocopy, recording, or any other—except for brief quotations in printed reviews without the prior permission of the publisher.

Published by Hypurpley Press, Tulsa, Oklahoma.

All rights reserved.

Up, Down, and All Around

A Parent's Handbook for Discipling Children According to Deuteronomy 6

Table of Contents

Chapter	Page
Introduction	9
1-Taste	16
2-Seek	21
3-Come	27
4-Believe	31
5-Confess	37
6-Follow	44
7-Read	47
8-Memorize	55
9-Pray — How to Pray	60
10-Pray — Lord's Prayer and Prayer Walking	67
11-Pray — God Answers	73
12-Thank	78
13-Attend	83
14-Bring	87
15-Worship Only God	92
16-Worship the Creator	98
17-Worship as a Living Sacrifice	103
18-Praise	109
19-Abide	113
20-Trust	118
21-Walk	123
22-Obey	127
23-Discern	133
24-Avoid	138
25-Rest	145
26-Remember	151
27-Know	156
28-Love God	161
29-Love People	167
30-Look at the Birds and Flowers	172
31-Tell	176

32-Keep - What is Good 181
33-Share 186
34-Plant 189
35-Listen 193
36-Look at the ants 198
37-Train 202
38-Build 206
39-Wait 210
40-Humble 215
41-Forgive 221
42-Heap 226
43-Keep – Your Word 231
44-Fix 235
45-Choose 239
46-Fan 244
47-Respect 248
48-Encourage 252
49-Celebrate 256
50-Serve 260
51-Stand 265
52-Expect 270
Index 273

Up, Down, and All Around:
A Handbook for Discipling our Children According to Deuteronomy 6

Introduction:

A little girl smudged with lipstick walking in her mommy's high heels, a little boy wearing daddy's ballcap and tool belt: this is a normal picture of our children imitating their parents. Discipling our kids is similar. They should begin mimicking what they see us doing in our Christian Walk. Children will imitate the worship practices they see before they really believe them or understand them. Discipleship with our children involves seeing them imitate our discipleship, then question it, and finally accept it as their own.

Most of the lessons in this book require very little preparation on your part. The very nature of discipling children means we seize the moments. So, that is how this book is written — in bite-sized lessons that can be used on a moment's notice. Each one emphasizes a verb we use in following Christ. Each lesson focuses on one of the areas mentioned in Deuteronomy 6.

> **You must love the LORD your God with all your heart, with all your soul, and with all your strength. Always remember these commands that I give you today. Be sure to teach them to your children. Talk about these commands when you sit in your house and when you walk on the road. Talk about them when you lie down and when you get up. Tie them on your hands and wear them on your foreheads to help you remember my teachings. Write them on the doorposts of your houses and on your gates.**
> **(Deuteronomy 6:5-9, ERV)**

We will cover all of these, emphasizing loving God and committing to Him completely. Some lessons will draw on nature and being outdoors while others can be done in the car while driving. We have bedtime lessons and breakfast table lessons as well as craft lessons that help us wear God's word or put it on the walls of our homes.

In addition, the lessons can be done in any order. Use them when they best fit the situation and mindset of your children. This book is meant to be a tool and blessing for you as you disciple your little ones.

Each lesson will have an icon letting you know which type of lesson it is:

When You Sit in Your House

    At the Table

    Anywhere at Home

    In the Bathtub

    Crafting at Home

When You Walk on the Road

    In the car

    In nature

    In the rain

When You Lie Down and When You Get Up

    At bedtime

    In the morning:

I've also included suggestions for picture books or board books that go along with each lesson (They don't call me the Picture Book Lady for nothing). The suggested books are not all Christian books, and they are a completely optional part of the lesson. The main purpose they serve is sparking more conversation about the topic during another part of the day or later in the week. Or we may want to start with the book and then go into the lesson. The hope is that reading the suggested book together might encourage our children to ask any questions or confirm understanding from the lesson.

Strength for the Parents:

The first part of each lesson is for us as parents. Whether you are a single parent, the only Christian in your home, or in a two-parent Christian home, these devotions are for us to be encouraged and check our hearts before we share the lesson. Our prayer and hope are that we all find words to spur us on in the adventure of walking with Christ and helping others including our children do the same.

In addition, the second section of each lesson includes some considerations we may need to think about in preparing to parent and teach our children. Sometimes these may not apply to our situation, but they are meant to prepare us a little more with some beneficial pointers in our parenting and discipleship of our children.

Keys to Discipling Children:

Taking advantage of teachable moments — Teaching children really requires a teachable moment radar. When a child is really listening and teachable, we must be ready to drop whatever we're doing and use that moment as the gift it is.

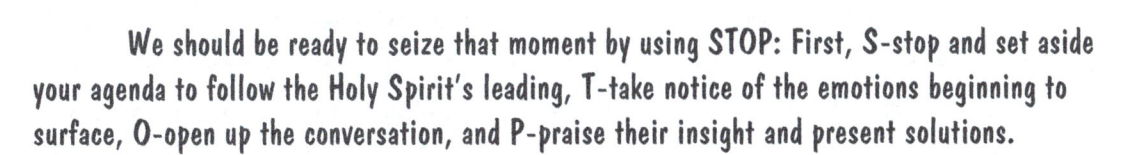

We should be ready to seize that moment by using STOP: First, S-stop and set aside your agenda to follow the Holy Spirit's leading, T-take notice of the emotions beginning to surface, O-open up the conversation, and P-praise their insight and present solutions.

Teachable moments by their nature are not expected and interrupt your daily plan or busy schedule. If we aren't willing to stop what we planned or what we're doing and seize that moment, it could be gone very quickly. That's why I use STOP as an acrostic to remind us.

S - As we **stop** and **shift** gears to make the most of the moment, we can ask questions for further understanding if our child has started by asking us something.

T - If we are dealing with a situation where our child is in pain or about to get into an argument, we can **take** notice of those emotions. Most of the time in teachable moments, emotions are involved. We want to get our children talking. We want to hear their hearts, their concerns, and understand what they are thinking so that we can address the situation accurately. If we jump to conclusions or offer quick solutions to what we think is the problem, our child won't feel heard, and the only thing they may learn is a feeling that they don't matter.

O - **Opening** up the conversation with our kids is always our goal. This is where the real discipleship takes shape. If we are doing all the talking, it's a lecture, not an interaction. Real learning is most often a part of interactive learning.

P - Finally, we need to take the time to **praise** and encourage. Our children can often surprise us with their insight or their misunderstandings. We need to encourage their critical thinking and their attempts at reasoning. If their thinking is misguided, we have the amazing opportunity to help them see the truth. It's so important. And if they have some great insights, it is a joy to encourage those thoughts. Either way, our children gain truth in the interaction and feel encouraged for trying.

Teaching them what we've learned — We cannot bring someone where we haven't been in our Christian walk, not well, anyway. When we've truly learned something, we can teach it. In Matthew, Jesus commanded us to make disciples teaching them to obey all He commanded us (Matthew 28:20). And Deuteronomy 6 makes it clear that we are teach our children repeatedly what God has taught us. This means we need to grow in our faith constantly and consistently. Then we can teach our children how to grow in theirs.

Testifying to what God has done in our lives — Like the examples in the Bible (Joshua 4 and Exodus 13, for instance) of children asking questions and the parents telling what God has done, we can do the same. When our children ask questions, we can share what God has done in our lives as well and help them remember who God is by what He has done. We help them see the relationship we have with God, that God is real and alive — not just a story in an old book. When we share our testimonies of God's work in our lives, we make Him real to our children and help them to know Him.

Talking and Listening — We can't catch the teachable moments (when our children are open to learning) and defining moments (when we share something with our children that helps them understand who they are) if communication is closed. We must talk to our kids and let them talk to us. As we listen, we learn where needs are and when teachable moments arise. We need to learn to use open-ended questions and to encourage our children to talk to us about anything and everything. This means we are thrilled (okay, maybe not always thrilled, but pleased) when they ask so. many. questions. When they hit their teenage years, you will be so grateful you've kept the dialogue open.

Transparently Telling the Truth — We cannot sugar-coat living this life. It's often difficult. If we aren't transparent about these things (in age-appropriate ways), we can set up our children for harder struggles in their walk with God. Jesus told us we'd have troubles in following Him; we need to pass the word along. We would see fewer young adults walking away from their faith if we had consistently been honest about the difficulties, about counting the cost of discipleship, and that we choose to follow Christ even when it's hard or painful. We want to be honest about the good news too: through it all, we have His peace, love, and joy. We love our kids when we tell them the truth.

With our youngest children we can begin by simply answering their questions and being honest. "Sometimes I'm afraid too. But the truth helps me face that fear and watch it disappear (sometimes). I pray and remember that God is always with me. I am never alone." Or "When I was little, I was afraid of the dark too. My mom let me have a nightlight, and that was all I needed. Would you like a nightlight?" When we are honest in age-appropriate ways, we lay the groundwork for tackling the harder questions as our children get older.

Another part of transparency, especially as our children get older, is to be transparent in acknowledging our mistakes. Especially as first-time parents, we may only focus on behavior modification — teaching what to do and not do, character traits rather than heart change. Let's be honest—we want to play the part of the Holy Spirit in our kids' lives sometimes. This, in some instances, can build resentment toward religion. If we find ourselves focusing more on behavior than true character and self-discipline, we can acknowledge that, talk to our kids about it, and help them understand our true goals in teaching them. We aren't looking for well-behaved children. We want Christ-following adults who have integrity, humility, and trust God with their lives, allowing the Holy Spirit to change their hearts. It's not always easy to be transparent about our hearts' desires for our kids or letting them know when we've messed up, but it can bless them and teach them so much about godly character and about the character of God.

I have not stopped thanking God for you. I pray for you constantly, asking God, the glorious Father of our Lord Jesus Christ, to give you spiritual wisdom and insight so that you might grow in your knowledge of God. I pray that your hearts will be flooded with light so that you can understand the confident hope he has given to those he called—his holy people who are his rich and glorious inheritance. I also pray that you will understand the incredible greatness of God's power for us who believe him. This is the same mighty power that raised Christ from the dead and seated him in the place of honor at God's right hand in the heavenly realms.
(Ephesians 1:16-20, NLT)

I pray this for you and for your children. I thank God you have accepted God's calling to disciple your children and to help raise up the next generation of Christ followers. We need wisdom. We need to grow in our faith and understanding. God is with us. He will help us. Daily, may we gain more understanding of God and His will and be able to pass that along to our children. God bless you, and may He open up many teachable and defining moments in your family.

One final note: I want to encourage you. Your desire to disciple your children is wonderful. These lessons are written out in an orderly fashion, but we soon learn to accept that life is messy, and kids are sometimes smarter than we think, and the lesson may go awry. I encourage you to roll with it. Have fun. Ask God to help you notice the learning that is taking place even if the dog knocks over the object lesson or your child knew the answer before you wanted them to. We aren't perfect, and neither are our amazing kids. But we are families seeking to follow the God we love and who loves us abundantly.

My mentor encouraged me one day when I was frazzled and discouraged. She had me stop and just look at my family in the other room. My kids were having fun. They were happy. There was a sense of family unity and contentment. She said, "You're doing great. Your kids are happy."

I encourage you to stop and look at your family. I pray God gives you eyes to see beyond the messiness of life and see the hearts of your children. And I pray he helps you see his heart for your children and for you. God bless you!

Terrie Hellard-Brown

Taste

For Mom and Dad
Preparing our Hearts

Scripture: Psalm 34:8-9; 1 Peter 2:1-4

Bubble tea is a popular drink in the US now, but it started in Taiwan. We had lived in Taiwan for a few years, and I had no desire to try that weird drink. It just sounded wrong. I didn't want to have to chew my drink, and I was sure I'd choke to death trying to master drinking milk tea and chewing the tapioca pearls. It just sounded wrong. But then, one day a friend convinced me to try it. It was delicious. It was addictive. Soon, I needed my Nai Cha (milk tea) fix every day like some people need their full caf latte.

When we started seeing Bobba shops open in the United States, our family was so excited. Two of my kids even got jobs working at one of the shops. It's silly, but it was like we were getting to experience *home* a little each time. That first drink always takes me back to our alley in Taiwan to my favorite tea shop. We are so homesick for Taiwan most of the time, and tasting milk tea somehow takes a little bit of the sting out of not being there.

I believe that's the experience the Psalmist spoke about in Psalm 34. When we taste and see that God is good, we are forever changed. We know him. We want to be with him. We know in every fiber of our being that he is good. And when we walk away, we miss him. Just as tasting involves our senses and emotions, knowing God reaches our intellect, emotions, spirit, and soul. Everything in our life changes.

I was very young when I started following Christ, but my husband was a senior in high school. He said that he went to bed that night with one set of friends, and when he woke up the day after answering God's call during the invitation at a Billy Graham crusade in Singapore, he woke up with a whole new set of friends. Christ had changed his life. His old friends pulled away, but his new friends embraced him as family. His mom tells how insecurities fell away, and he literally came to life.

Peter recognized that tasting the goodness of God would change us in a similar way. Knowing God leads us to faithfulness and gives us new life in Christ. Peter calls us to put away the things of our old nature and of the world and choose to follow Jesus faithfully.

I love that scripture connects knowing God to our sense of taste because when we know the taste of something, we never forget it. We can just think of the food, and we remember the taste. It's a very personal experience that stays with us forever.

Once we know God, we are changed forever. We know his character, his voice, his heart. We never forget that experience. We may stray from him, but we still remember what it was like to feel his presence and to be close to him, and longing for that relationship helps draw us back to him.

When we taste God's goodness, we also experience a taste of heaven. We become homesick for a place we've never been. First Peter 1:8 talks about having faith without seeing Christ, and Ephesians 1 talks about living in heavenly places. God is so good that he allows us to experience the comfort of heaven in our lives now even though we are so imperfect and are surrounded by such a messed up world. The joy and hope that experience brings us is immeasurable. We can't help but praise God and thank him for his goodness.

Prayer: We should spend time thanking God for his goodness and for how he has forever changed our lives. We can also thank God that if a child or loved one has strayed far from God, he draws them back. We can keep praying for them and rejoice that God never lets go of anyone. We can also thank God that we get to experience a little of heaven here as we taste and see that God is good.

Preparing to Parent

One of the skills we want our children to learn is how to interpret scripture properly. These verses give us a good example of figurative language used in the poetry of scripture. Some scripture, like Genesis and the Gospels are actual events that took place. Some of the books are laws or rules to follow. And some parts of scripture are figurative metaphors like saying we can taste God or that Jesus is a rock (1 Peter 2:4).

You may want to choose some specific verses to share with your children, and allow them to say whether they are real events/people/rules or if they are metaphors or figurative language.

Some examples:
Genesis 1:3; Luke 19:38-40; Luke 19:41-42; Numbers 22:21-31; John 10:7-9; Isaiah 55:12; Hebrews 13:5

For the Family
Enjoying the Lesson Together

Scripture: Psalm 34:8-9; 1 Peter 2:3
(remember to choose a verse as your family memory verse with each lesson)

Object Lesson: Yummy Dinner

Prepare a delicious dinner. Put plates of food in front of each child, but don't let them start eating. After prayer, tell them you want to share something with them before they eat.

Read the verses together.

Ask the children how their food tastes. They should object saying they haven't tasted it yet, so they don't know if it is good.

Affirm that they are correct. How will they find out if the food is good? By tasting it.

Have them take a taste and tell you now if it is good.

Ask how we can know that God is good. In a sense we taste God because we've experienced him in our lives. As we experience him, we learn that he is good and loving. In this way, we have learned about him and know him.

While you finish eating dinner together, ask them to think about what they know about God.

If possible, have a whiteboard or poster board that you can write on after dinner. Each person should share what they know about God. He is good, loving, kind, trustworthy, omniscient, omnipresent, powerful...

Prayer/Song/Poem: Each person should say a sentence prayer thanking God for his goodness and praising him for who he is.

Activity: Tasting Jelly Bellies and Demonstrating God's Presence

Tasting Jelly Bellies can just be fun to taste and see IF it is good. We can't tell just by looking at them. They are all very pretty, but once we taste, we know for sure. With God, every time we experience him, we learn he is good, and we learn more about how he is good as we learn more about him. We grow more and more in our faith and love for him by learning more and more about him.

Using a bowl of water, a glass cup, and a piece of paper can demonstrate how that even though we can't see God, he is still there.

Have the bowl of water in front of you.
Show the children the empty glass and ask if there is anything in it. They will probably say no, nothing is in it.

Then, wad up the piece of paper and put it in bottom of the glass. Make sure it won't move when you turn the glass over.

Carefully, with the glass straight up and down, put the glass in the bowl upside down. (if it's done right, the air in the glass will keep the water away from the paper).

Make sure the children can confirm that the glass is totally submerged in the water.

Pull out the glass and show the children that the paper is still dry. How is that possible?

Because the glass was not really empty. It was filled with air, and the air stopped the water from getting to the paper.

In a similar way we know that God is everywhere even when we can't see him. Because he loves us, he promises that he is always be with us and will never leave us. He goes with us. He protects us. He helps us.

Picture Books: *Quinn's Promise Rock* by Christie Thomas, *What Is God Like?* by Beverly Lewis, *The God Contest* by Carl Laferton

Seek

For Mom and Dad
Preparing our Hearts

Scripture: Psalm 119:2; 2 Chronicles 7:14; Psalm 63:1; Acts 17:27; 2 Chronicles 15:1-7; James 4:4-10; Matthew 6:33

Have you ever seen a small child looking for a parent? My son would start the "Mom, Mom, Mom, Mom" routine while he was looking, and even when I said, "Yes, what do you need?" He would continue calling "Mom." It used to make us laugh. He would finally say, "Oh!" and tell me what he needed.

I think sometimes we are that way with God. Several scriptures tell us to seek God and to search for him diligently. It is part of repentance and intention in our walk with God. We are seeking him, desiring to spend time with him, and purposefully wanting to follow him. It's not that he's hiding from us, but we've wandered away or lost sight of him by focusing on other things or being busy or whatever has distracted us. Just like we aren't usually hiding from our children when they come looking for us, God is not hiding from us.

The truth is, if we must seek God, we have wandered away from him. He is not hiding. He is always with us, but we've lost sight of him for whatever reason. We've focused on the things of this world or willfully chosen to sin. We need to seek God and draw near to him. He is there, and he wants to draw near to us once again.

We cannot love this world and love God at the same time. We cannot seek the world and seek God at the same time. Jesus said in Matthew 6 that we cannot serve two masters. On this journey we call discipleship, we choose to follow Christ in obedience and holiness which means we seek him and his kingdom alone, not him and his kingdom and this world.

Prayer: If we find ourselves feeling far from God or like we've wandered from the path of faithfully following him, he is only a prayer away. We can humble ourselves and pray, turn away from our selfish ways to where he awaits. We can have renewed fellowship with him now, in this moment, if we will just seek him with all our hearts.

Preparing to Parent

We want to help our children find God. We want to lead them in truth and see them choose to follow him with their whole hearts, and it is a daunting task. We can feel overwhelmed at times like we are not up for the mission, and we are tempted to let their Sunday School teachers and other church family lead them.

However, we know in our heart of hearts that God has given us these little ones to guide and nurture. We can pick up this mantel he's given us, and with his Spirit leading us, we can help our children as they seek God. We can disciple them beginning with teaching them who God is, how to find him, and leading them to follow him in faith.

The wonderful part of parents discipling their own children is that we know them better than anyone else other than God. We can apply Proverbs 22:6 in their education and in their spiritual training. We can teach them the way that God intends them to go. We are more aware of how they are receiving the lessons and stories they are learning from the Bible. If a child is sensitive, we can help them understand correctly what the lesson is teaching.

For instance, if they feel God is unfair in sending Adam and Eve out of the garden, we can help them understand the magnitude of our sin and the consequences of it. Or if they feel he is unfair for punishing Adam when Eve handed him the fruit, we can help them see that Adam was there with her. He listened to the serpent but said nothing. He ignored his responsibilities, and he should have tried to stop her. They were both supposed to tend the garden, yet Satan was in the middle of it.

In a classroom, the teacher tries to answer each child's questions and check for understanding, but that teacher can't usually do it as well as we can sitting with our child in the car, the park, or at the dinner table.

So, we can feel encouraged and empowered to take on this wonderful calling to lead our children as they seek the Lord. We need to take them to church, and let their lives be enriched by the family they find there, but we must also step up and fulfill this blessed calling God has given us called parent.

For the Family
Enjoying the Lesson Together

Scripture: Psalm 119:2; Acts 17:27; Psalm 63:1; Jeremiah 29:13
(remember to choose a verse as your family memory verse with each lesson)

Object Lesson: Seeking Tangram Puzzle Pieces

If you have tangram blocks, you will need a set for each child. Hide the pieces around the room for each child to find. Since each block is a different color, when they find two red ones, they can give one to their sibling.

If you don't have tangram blocks, you can copy and cut out the pieces in this lesson. Use card stock or laminate the pieces.

For younger children, you may want to hide a whole set in a baggie for the child to find.

Once they find the pieces, they can use the pattern example to make the puzzle. You can find other designs for free online that use the same set of puzzle pieces to create animals and objects.

After they create the heart, share the scriptures and talk about what it means to seek God and why we seek him. Help them understand that it doesn't mean he is hiding and doesn't want to be found like a game of hide-and-seek, but that he desires to know we want to know him. He loves us and wants a relationship with us.

If your children helped each other find the pieces or you helped them find the pieces, share how we help others find Jesus. And that's what you are doing in teaching them about God too.

As you end the object lesson, if your child does not have his or her own Bible, this would be a great time to give them one and tell them how they can find God in his word. Reading and learning the Bible is one of the main ways we seek God.

Prayer/Song/Poem: Share the song "Small and Simple Faith" by Angie Killian Music or "Come Meet Jesus" by Mary Rice Hopkins

Activity: Play a fun game of hide-and-seek

A second activity would be to visit a farmer's market and give your children a scavenger hunt list to find at the market.

Then, when you finish, you can talk about the fruit of the Spirit from Galatians 5. When we find God and follow him, our lives start to show it by the fruit in our lives. It's not that we have to make ourselves love others, fight so hard to be patient, or grit our teeth to pretend to be joyful. Trees and plants don't strain to bear fruit. It just grows because of the nutrients they receive. God's fruit grows in our lives when we have found him and let him grow in our lives.

Picture Books: *Seek and Find: New Testament Bible Stories* by Sarah Parker, *Those Who Seek God* by Niki Milburn, *Chasing God's Glory* by Dorina Lazo Gilmore-Young

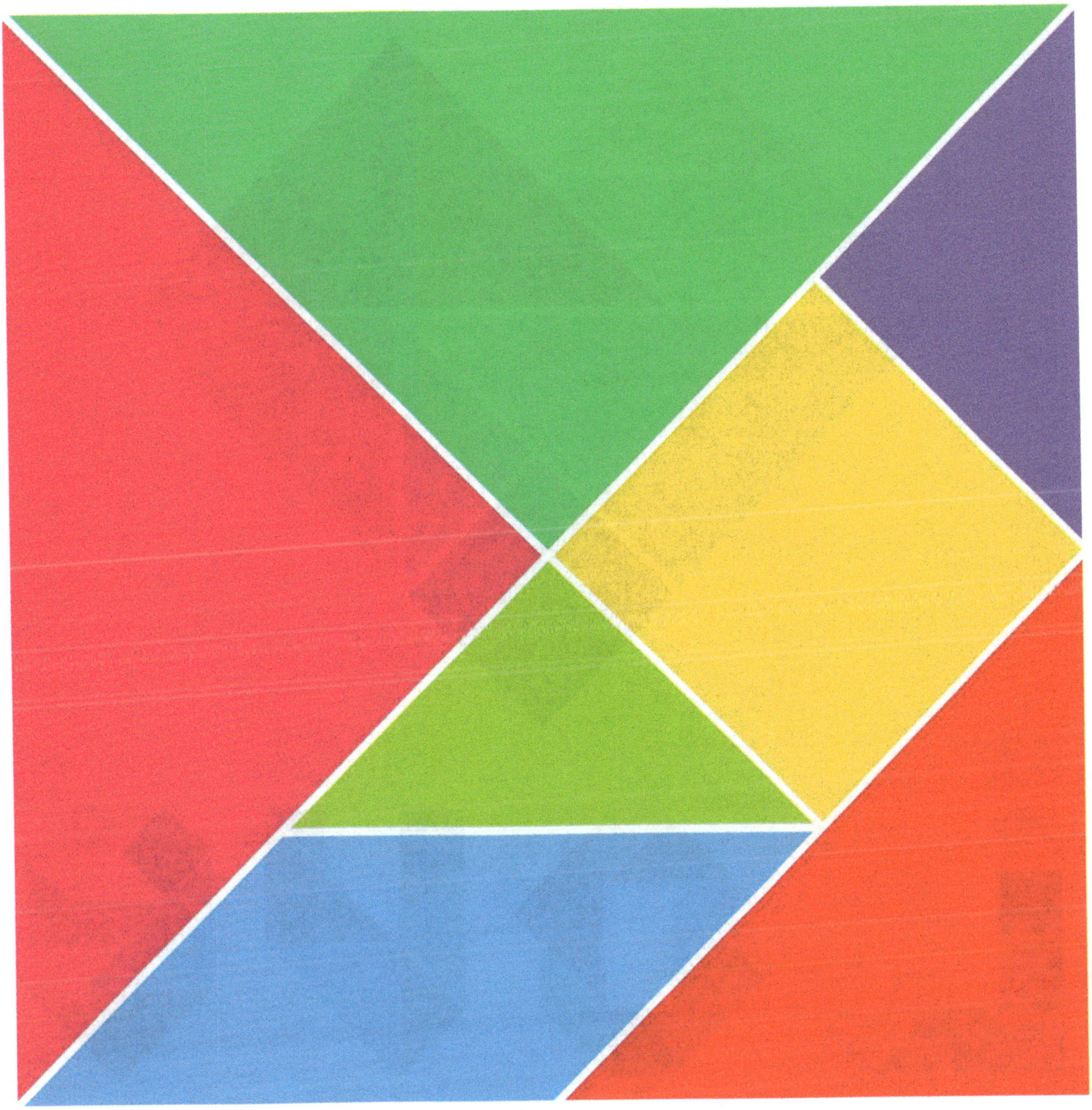

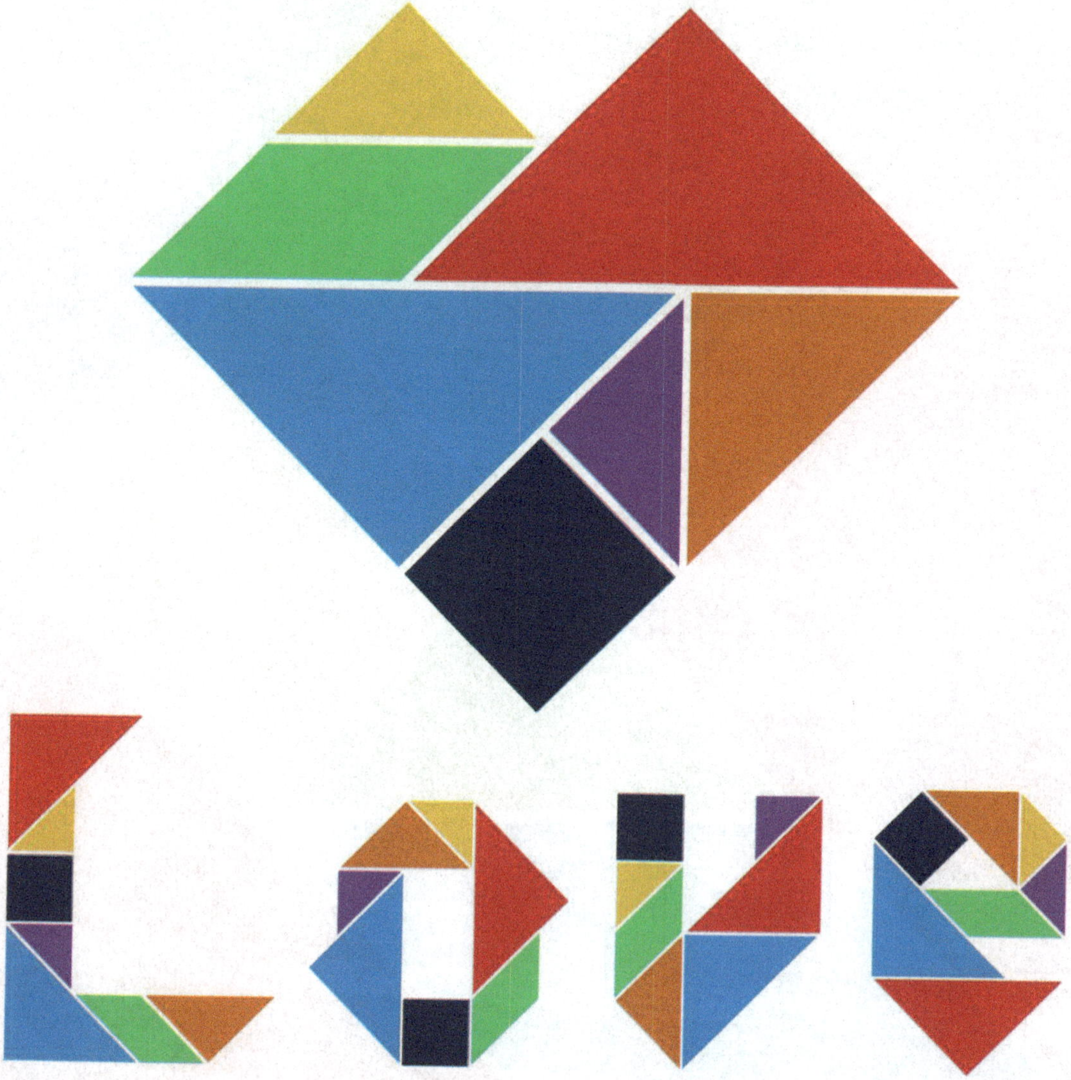
Love

Come

For Mom and Dad
Preparing our Hearts

Scripture: James 4:8; Matthew 11:28

I do tend to overcommit which is a common problem for most pastor's wives. When being so busy, I can get caught up in the doing of ministry rather than the being with God and knowing God. I realized that years ago when I had gone through a particular week doing ministry day after day, but I had not sat down with my Bible and spent time with God alone in a meaningful way. I felt disconnected from God and worn out, stressed, and just flat. I remember the amazing restorative power of opening the Bible and reading, feeling God's presence, and a sense of peace and calm washing over me. It was like sitting outside on a cool day with a soft breeze blowing past and just breathing in joy.

When God calls us to come to him, to draw near, it is not a demanding command, but a gentle calling to rest and restoration. He knows we need time away from everything to just be in his presence and to know that he is God. I think of Genesis before the fall when the voice of God walked with Adam and Eve in the cool of the evening. That time, in that perfection of how life was meant to be, is a beautiful picture of peace, rest, and restoration after a long day of work.

We all need time with God. We all need to lay down the burdens of life and take up the good works God has for us to do. We need to lay down the troublesome and sinful thoughts that bombard our minds and allow God to graciously renew our minds and fill them with praise and thoughts that honor him.

Prayer: Spend time just resting in God's presence and letting him minister to you today. Bring your concerns, your burdens, and any sins to him, and leave them at his feet. End with praise and thanksgiving.

Preparing to Parent

One of the points we want to make sure our children understand is that God calls us to come to him just as we are. We don't have to make ourselves better or wait until we do better to come to him. This is especially important once they are believers, and they sin. The enemy tries to tell us to stay away from God because he is disappointed in us or can't use us, that our lives are too horrible, and we are too defective. We need to help our children understand that as soon as they realize they have sinned, they need to repent and turn back to God. We must help them realize that even if they feel guilty, they should turn back to God immediately. Ask God for forgiveness, get things right, and don't wait.

For the Family
Enjoying the Lesson Together

Scripture: James 4:8; Matthew 11:28
(remember to choose a verse as your family memory verse with each lesson)

Object Lesson: An Invitation

Supplies: Invitations

Get a simple invitation to an event. You can make one or buy one or share one from a previous event. You may want to even create one for a fun event you've decided to have for your family or the neighborhood children. That is up to you. But whatever you do, talk about what an invitation means. Ask about what we do when we get an invitation.

Read the verses and discuss what kinds of invitations God gives us.

Prayer/Song/Poem: Some beautiful songs have been written sharing the message of "Come Just As You Are." My favorite is Crystal Lewis's from several years ago. However, you may want to teach your children the traditional hymn "Just As I Am."

Activity: Plan a party and make invitations.

Here are a few ideas for some parties with a Christian theme. See what you and your family can come up with.

The B-I-B-L-E Party — each guest brings something that refers to a description of God's word such as a lamp, bread, etc. For one of the games, make a treasure hunt, and the treasure might include some Bibles, pamphlets, or Christian books along with snacks or candy.

Favorite Bible Character Party — this is a costume party, and each child tells why they are dressed as they are, why that character is their favorite. One of the party games could be to have a picture taken next to a life-sized replica of Goliath; pin the tail on Balaam's donkey; and a Run the Hebrews 12 Race.

Celebrating Friendship — This party is an ice cream social. For a craft, use the pattern at the end of this chapter. Have each child write a word description of what makes a good friend on the ice cream scoop and glue the scoop to their paper cones. Also, create an ice cream cone graphic for each attendee and set one at each place at the table. Each person will then go around to write kind messages to encourage the other attendees (sort of like signing a High School yearbook). After this, make ice cream sundaes together. If you want to add another element to the party, you can make homemade ice cream, and talk about what ingredients make a friendship.

Your family may have some other fun ideas. But whatever you choose, pray about ways to tell others about coming to Jesus.

Picture Books: *The Awesome Super Fantastic Forever Party* by Joni Eareckson Tada, *The Big Wide Welcome* by Trillia Newbell, *The Man in the Tree and the Brand New Start* by Carl Laferton; *Little Mole Gives Thanks* by Gleny Nellist

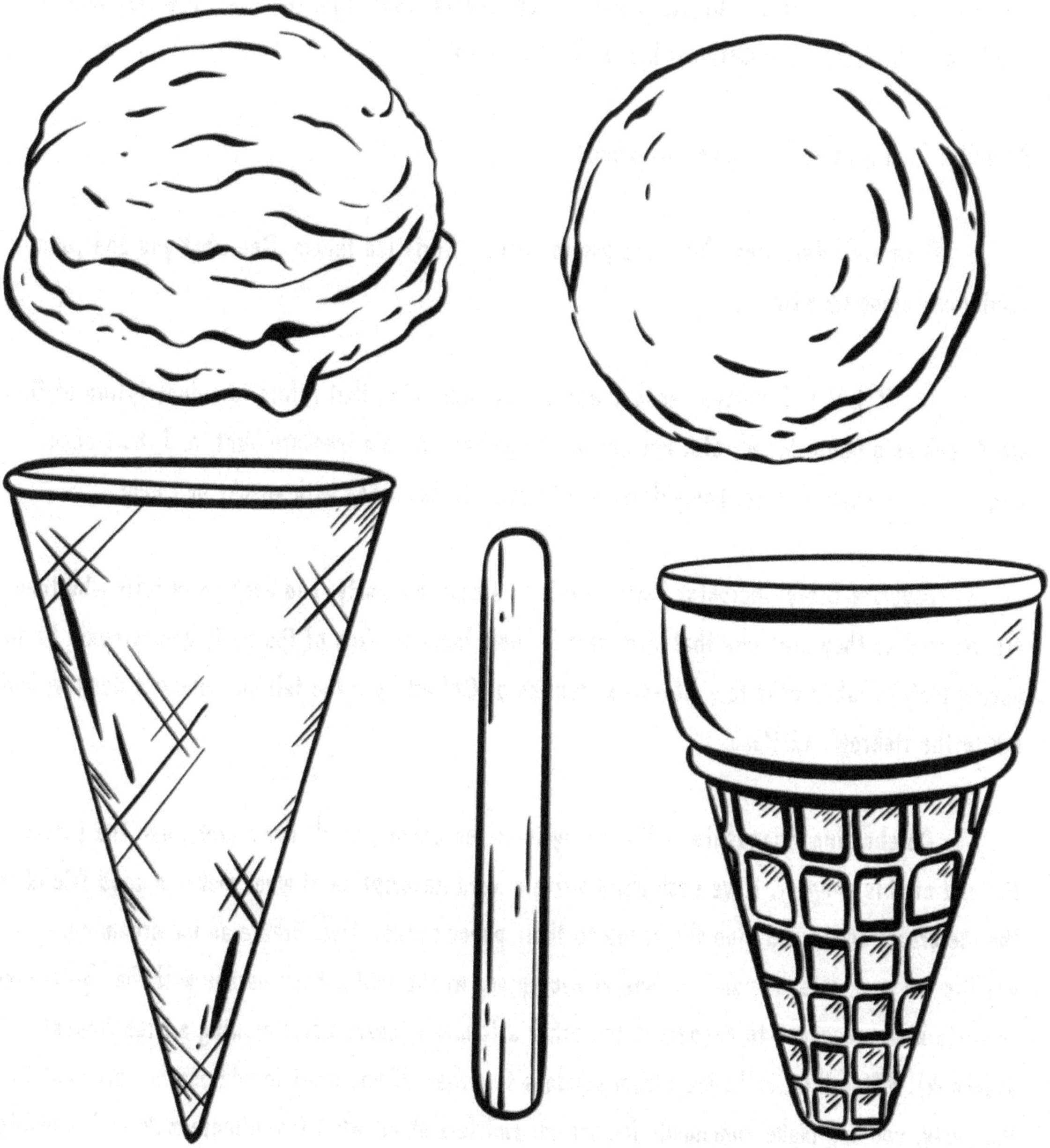

Believe

For Mom & Dad:
Preparing Our Hearts

Scripture: Ephesians 2:8-9

As a kid, I was gullible. I believed what people told me, especially my mom. But my mom had a sense of humor I didn't quite understand at the age of five. I told her I saw spots when I looked at a lightbulb. She told me I might need glasses. She was teasing, but it went right over my head, and it backfired. Not only was I gullible, but I liked to share EVERYTHING with my kindergarten teacher. My mom was so embarrassed when she found out I told my teacher I might need glasses because I saw spots after looking at a lightbulb.

In the Christian Church we talk a lot about believing. Thankfully, we can trust God and believe what he says even when it seems impossible because with God, all things are possible. What we believe about God affects how we interact with Him and how we behave in our lives.

We can ask God to help us examine our hearts and minds. Do we truly believe Jesus completely paid the penalty for our sin? Do we believe we are unable to earn our salvation in any way? Or do we realize we are still striving trying to make God love us more? Do we rest in His love and provision or still strive to earn His favor? Do we struggle with our failures and feel condemned even though we know Jesus paid for all our sin?

We really must get these questions of faith settled in our hearts and minds. Too many Christians continue to strive and try to earn their salvation even though we all say we believe our faith in Christ has saved us, and we sing "Jesus paid it all."

Our service and ministry should be an outflow of our salvation, not an effort to earn it. (Ephesians 2:10)

Receive His peace in the knowledge that you are completely saved.

You may want to worship and pray listening to songs like:

"Yet Not I But Through Christ in Me" by CityAlight

"Completely Done" by Sovereign Grace Music

"Be Still, Be Still, My Soul (Psalm 46)" by Sovereign Grace Music

Prayer: Let's ask God to renew our minds helping us to hold on to what is true. We are not God and we can never be perfect this side of heaven. It is only His grace that saves us and gives us His perfect love and gives us a relationship with Him. He calls us to be still (Psalm 46:10) and to rest (Matthew 11:28-30). He tells us that we are not condemned but are completely His child (John 3:18, Romans 8:1).

God, help us see where we are striving in our strength instead of resting in Yours. Show us when we shift from trusting You to trying to earn Your favor.

Preparing to Parent

Two things we must be aware of in parenting our children through the concepts in this lesson:

1. Are we showing them that we trust God, or are we demonstrating a religion of works?
2. Are we showing grace to our children, or are we parenting with a works-based, conditional love?

This is difficult, and so convicting when we are confronted with where we may have failed in this area. But we can take heart. No one is alone by any means. We have all struggled in this area. However, we don't want to continue this way, and the only way to break free is with God's help.

We must earnestly pray, asking for the Lord's wisdom and the Holy Spirit's guidance especially in this area of our own lives and our parenting.

We serve an awesome, loving, merciful God who loves us and our kids more than we can grasp. If we seek Him, He will lead us.

For the Family:
Enjoying the Lesson Together

Scripture: John 3:1-18; 1 Peter 1:23; 2 Corinthians 5:17
(choose a verse as your family memory verse with each lesson)

Object Lesson: Bullfrogs and Butterflies

If you can find some chrysalises or tadpoles, that's awesome. But you may just go to a pond and see frogs or toads or to the park or your backyard and see butterflies. Whichever you find, spend some time watching them and talking about them, and then discuss the process of metamorphosis.

Our word for today is BELIEVE. What does that mean?

When we believe some things, we can be very wrong. If I believe I can fly, and I jump in the air, what is going to happen?

We're talking about frogs and butterflies today because they change or are "born again" as a new creature from a tadpole to a frog or from a caterpillar to a butterfly.

What if a caterpillar believed really hard and tried with all his might, could he suddenly become a bird? That's right — believing the wrong thing won't help us no matter how hard we believe it. We must believe what's right. The caterpillar can become a butterfly if he does it right (which he does because God made him to know exactly what to do to become a butterfly). And we can be born again if we have correct thinking and believe what's right.

We can't just hope and believe we're good and are okay.

We must believe in the truth, and the truth is found in the Bible.

Our verses today tell us that we must believe and be born again. Nicodemus was confused about what Jesus meant. Is it confusing to you too? What about it seems confusing? What did God mean when he said we must be born again or that we become a new creation?

Why do we need to be born again?

Tadpoles and caterpillars look different on the outside when they change, but people mostly look different on the inside because their hearts are filled with God's love and forgiveness. How does having God's love and forgiveness make us look different on the outside?

We are changed when we believe in Jesus. What does that mean to you?

(Mom and Dad, share your stories of how Jesus changed your lives.)

What God does in our lives when we choose to believe and follow Him is just as miraculous as the caterpillar becoming a butterfly or a tadpole becoming a frog. We are totally new inside. We are forgiven from all our sin. We are a new person and live to know and follow God. It's the best, most wonderful miracle God does.

The Bible tells us that everyone has sinned, and it's separated us from God. What does sin mean?

We want to love God and know Him. We want Him to be pleased with us. That means something must change. That means we need to become new creations by being born again.

Do you know how we do that?

First, we know we need forgiveness for the wrong things we've done. So, we ask God to forgive us and make our lives clean and right with Him.

Second, we believe and follow God. When we believe in Jesus, we become a Christian or a person who follows Jesus. We choose to follow Jesus from now on, learning what the Bible says, praying, and getting to know God more and more. When we know Him, He helps us be kind, loving, patient, and good because His Spirit lives in us and is with us always. We aren't trying to be good. He makes us good by His Holy Spirit. He has changed us into a new person in Christ.

We may not change from a tadpole to a frog or a caterpillar to a butterfly, but we change from someone who isn't living for God to someone who is. We become His child whom He dearly loves, and we love and follow Him.

What do you think about that?
What questions do you have?

(With children, you usually don't have to ask if they want to become a Christian. If they are ready, they will usually tell you, but obey the Holy Spirit. If you feel you should ask, then ask. Otherwise, let your child show you where they are in their understanding and if they are ready to follow Christ).

Prayer: Pray thanking Jesus for saving you and making you new. Pray that each child will someday decide to follow Jesus too. (If your child is ready, help them pray to accept Christ's forgiveness and to express their commitment to follow Jesus).

Activity: Finger play (butterfly)

(Hands together with pointer fingers out)
Caterpillar squirms and crawls on the leaves and ground
(Pull fingers into hands and make a chrysalis)
He goes inside his chrysalis and changes do abound
(Open hands keeping first fingers interlocked and move hands like wings)
One day he comes back outside and begins to fly around
No longer a caterpillar, but a butterfly is found

Origami (jumping frog)

Get a sheet of square paper (if you can get origami paper, it works best)
This same design is on YouTube if you want to watch the steps on video

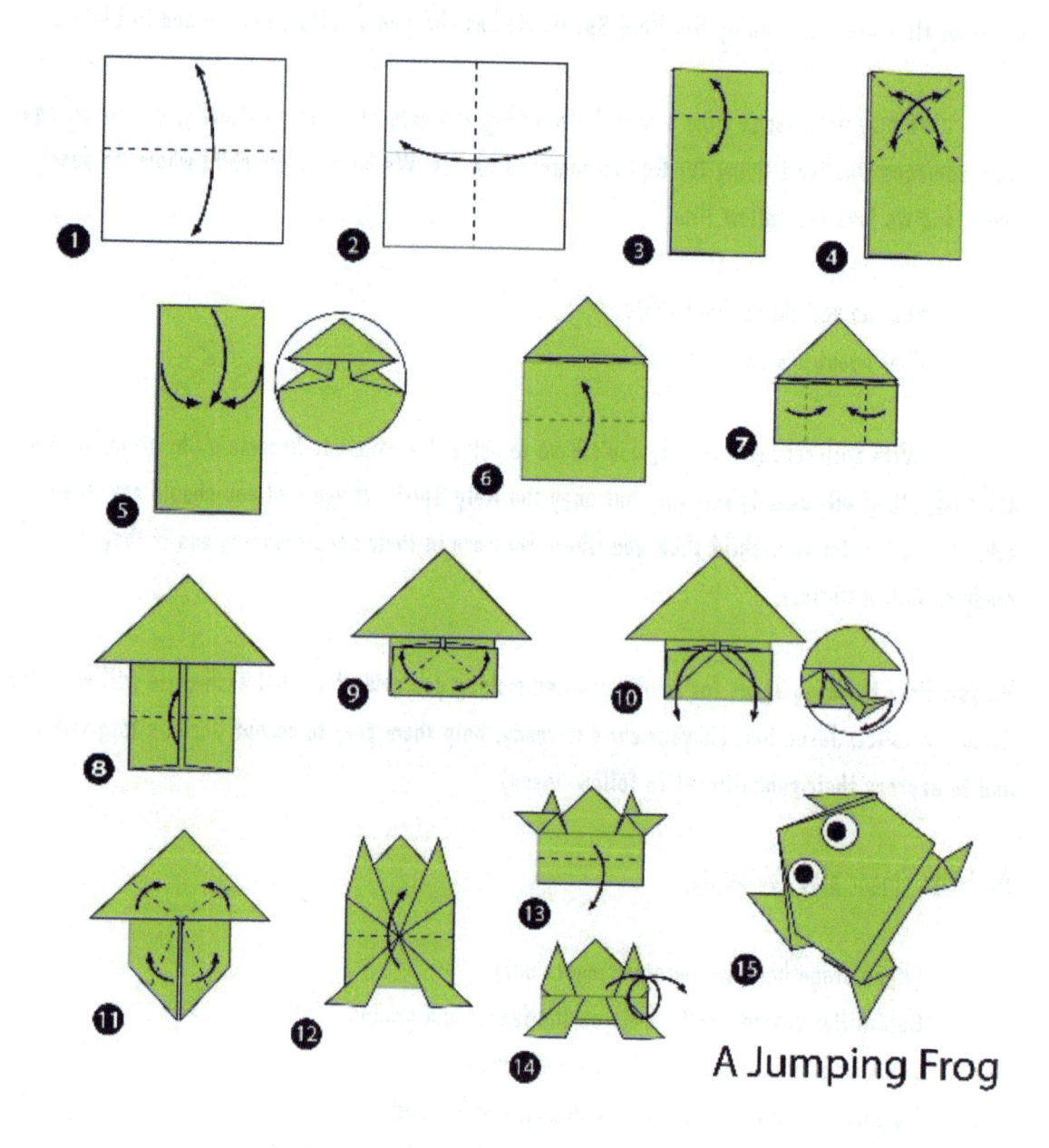

A Jumping Frog

Picture Books: *The Very Impatient Butterfly* by Ross Burach; *Ribbit: The Truth about Frogs* by Annette Whipple; *999 Tadpoles* by Ken Kimura, *Velma Gratch and the Way Cool Butterfly* by Alan Madison

Confess

For Mom and Dad
Preparing Our Hearts

Scripture: James 5:16

I walked through a very hard time in my Christian faith where I kept falling into the same sin over and over. I felt like I had no control over the temptation. It was always on my mind because I was filled with guilt and wanted to hide that I was struggling. But something miraculous happened when I finally confessed this sin to my husband and a couple women in our church. I wanted their prayer, so I finally asked for their help. But when I confessed my sin to them, suddenly it had no power over me. The fear and shame had kept me under the influence of that sin, but once I let go of hiding and confessed, the hold was gone. I was free and forgiven!

I learned through that situation that not everyone is able to be as kind and helpful as others are. One of the ladies never treated me the same after my confession; whatever her reasons, it was painful to experience. But even so, it felt worth the trial to be free from constant shame and guilt.

James 5:16 is a powerful verse. We've often heard, "Confession is good for the soul." The Bible basically says that it is vital to becoming a born-again soul. In addition to that, I would like to say that confession can be good for the marriage as well. If you are a single parent, I encourage you to find a person you can trust to be able to confess to and who will pray for you.

In the lesson on "Avoid" we talk about how confession helps us avoid temptation. It literally extinguishes Satan's fiery darts. We've especially seen this between husbands and wives. When we're tempted, we can confess it to our spouse. When we've failed, we can confess it. If you have trouble being that open with each other, or if either spouse deals with insecurities or jealousy, depending on the temptation, spouses may need to talk to another person they trust in their church, someone who has discipled them or an elder. However, if spouses can pray with each other and ask God to build their relationship so that they can trust one another and believe in each other enough, they'll likely find this kind of intimacy will draw them closer together.

Because confession and prayer bring a kind of intimacy and familiarity to a relationship, you will probably find it best, if you are not married, to find a confidante who is the same sex as you are, and especially if your confidante is married to someone else. You may also find having someone a little older than you helps too.

Harboring guilt, sin, or shame in our hearts and in our marriage will eventually cause a wedge between us. Satan will use it to tear marriages apart if he can.

Even for the single parent, Satan will use unresolved sin or habitual sin to tear you down as a believer and make it harder for you to lead your children in their faith.

Sin hurts relationships, all relationships from our relationship with God to those around us. Even when God has forgiven us, we may find it difficult to find victory. Confession helps in two main ways: we're no longer hiding what need confession, which often builds shame and we now have a partner who can pray for us and hold us accountable. Satan's schemes are thwarted, and we can begin to walk in victory.

If you are the one having trouble hearing about your spouse's temptations or sins—pray. Pray that you can support your spouse as he or she works through whatever is causing problems. Pray that you can forgive and not hold this against them. We must recognize that we are all sinners, and we are all weak at times. We can all fall into everyday temptations and even get trapped in addiction if we are not careful. So, first we must humble ourselves before God. Then, we must recognize the trust and transparency our spouse is showing us when confessing to us.

They are vulnerable like never before when sharing these struggles. It is never easy. Then, we seek God's heart and ask Him to help us respond in a godly manner. We can be our spouse's biggest fan and supporter by encouraging them as they walk away from whatever sin may be troubling them.

If you are the one facing temptation, especially if it is a habitual or constant temptation, you must seriously guard your heart. Talk with your spouse about how to keep yourself away from the temptation. Ask God to help you find victory in His strength and power. We are weak and feeble without God, and we must rely on his strength.

Confession, and the openness it requires, builds oneness with each other.

Prayer: If we are experiencing fear or shame, we need to pray for God to help us find someone to whom we can confess our sins, someone who will support us and help hold us accountable. If we are experiencing guilt or conviction of the Holy Spirit, we should immediately confess our sins to the Lord. He will set us free from our sins and renew our closeness to him.

Preparing to Parent

Confession is not a large part of most of our cultures. Even the type of confession seen in the Catholic church when people confess to their priest is not the same as what we're practicing here or what we want our children to embrace. The person we are sharing with is not absolving us of our sin, but is agreeing to walk alongside us in prayer and encouragement as we grow closer to God and truly forsake our sin.

We have an opportunity to create a culture in our homes where confession and reconciliation is a natural part of family life. Our homes should be a safe place where we can share our hurts and struggles. As parents, we must make it a priority because it won't happen naturally.

Some points to consider whether your children understand this concept:

Even when we confess to someone, we still need to pray and confess to God and ask for His forgiveness too.

Confessing when they've done something wrong may result in lesser punishment, but it does not do away with all consequences necessarily.

All family members may need to confess sin at different times, even parents, especially if we have wronged our children.

Responses from family members should be gracious and not angry or shaming. (If we cannot respond that way, we let the person know we need some time to process what they've said, and we will meet back to talk about it later in the day or the next day).

We promise not to yell or lecture, although we may need to talk further about the situation or how to prevent it from happening again.

If the child is resistant when we are trying to talk with them about next steps or changes, they may need to spend some time praying alone about why they are feeling the way they are---why are they resistant? Where are they harboring pride or sin? (Parents may need to help younger children understand pride or describe sin as when we do something we know we shouldn't do).

No matter what, they can never do something so bad that we will not still love them and care about them. It is the same with God. He will always love us even when we fail or make choices that go against His commands.

The most harmful thing any of us can do is try to hide our sin or lie about it—even to ourselves.

Confession helps begin the healing process and wipes the slate clean.

For the Family
Enjoying the Lesson Together

Scripture: James 5:16; 1 John 1:9; Romans 3:23-24

(remember to choose a verse as your family memory verse with each lesson)

Object Lesson: Getting Clean

Dirt is the object for the lesson. So, you can choose to play in the mud before bathtime and get really dirty, or you may want to focus on dirty toys. Whatever you choose, we're talking about washing away the "dirt" and guilt of sin.

When we follow Jesus we try hard not to sin, but sometimes we mess up. Sometimes we choose to disobey Mom and Dad or God, and that means we sin. We may get mad and break something or hurt someone's feelings. When we do these things, we must confess our sins.

Do you know what happens when we confess our sins? They get washed away.

Today, we got really dirty. We want to get clean, so let's see what we can do.

Using a dry cloth, try to wipe away all the dirt.

Hmm. You are still dirty. No matter how much I try, I can't clean the dirt off of you.

What do we usually do when we get dirty?

That's right, we take a bath. And the water and soap washes away all the dirt, and we are like new, like we never got dirty in the first place. Isn't that wonderful?

(after the bath) How do you feel now that you are all clean from your bath?

Why did you need a bath? (depending how they answer, keep going) I had mud all over me.

How did you get mud on you? I tried to be careful, but it just got all over me.

You mean, you were just sitting there, and the mud jumped on you? How terrible! Jumping mud is very dangerous. No, I was playing in the mud and got dirty.

Oh! So if we play in the dirt and mud, we get dirty, right? Yes.

Now, if Mom or Dad had said don't play in the mud, but you did it anyway, that would mean you sinned. This time, we were playing in the mud for fun, but when we need to stay clean or are wearing our good clothes, we know we should not get that dirty. That's when it is wrong. How would you feel if that happened? Bad.

How can we feel better again? When we do something wrong, we sometimes feel dirty or guilty on the inside. We can't wash that away by ourselves. Jesus is the only one who can do that.

The Bible tells us exactly what to do. We confess our sins. Do you know what confess means? It means to admit we have done something wrong without blaming others; and when we can do that God is faithful and forgives us. It's like he gives us a bath and makes us clean. Isn't that wonderful? Nothing else can get rid of our sin. Just like the mud you had that we can't make go away. Only God can make it go away, and He does that when we confess our sins. When God forgives us, we aren't muddy anymore.

Part of our prayer time is confessing our sins. Each day, we should check our hearts and see if we have sinned and confess that to God. It's like taking your bath each night or washing your hands before we eat. And when you know you did something wrong, you should confess that immediately. If you hurt someone's feelings, you should confess to them first, and then to God. Ask your friend to forgive you first, and then ask God to forgive you. Even if your friend didn't forgive you, God will.

Sometimes when we do wrong, we want to hide it. We are afraid to tell anyone what we did. When we do that, you know what? We are just making ourselves miserable. It's like continuing to wear dirty clothes until you smell all stinky and no one wants to be your friend. It's just awful. So, instead of staying dirty, guilty, and miserable, we admit we've done wrong and ask God to forgive us.

You want to know a wonderful secret? When you get out of the bathtub, sometimes there is a ring of dirt left in the tub. Have you ever noticed that? If we didn't clean the tub, it would be disgusting after a while. But with God, it's different. When He forgives us, He cleanses us, and the sin is gone! He removes it so far away from us, He says He chooses to forget it as though we never did it. (Ps. 103:12; Hebrews 8:12).

Prayer/Song/Poem: Confess your sins to each other
　　　　　　　　　　Lean on God's word for truth
　　　　　　　　　　Exit tempting situations
　　　　　　　　　　Accept God's gift of grace and forgiveness
　　　　　　　　　　Next time, choose the right way

Activity: Dissolving sins
　　　　This activity requires buying dissolving paper (about $10-12 on Amazon). Each child and parent can write down their sins and ask God for forgiveness. When they do, they put the paper into a bowl of water (it seems that slightly warm water works a little faster). The paper and the list of sins disappears quickly.

　　　　Share the verse Micah 7:19.

Picture Books: (These are the same as the "Avoid" lesson) *Arlo and the Great Big Cover-Up* by Betsy Childs Howard, *Broken: The Problem of Sin* by Floyd Gary Pierce, *Don't Blame the Mud: Only Jesus Makes Us Clean* by Marty Machowski

Follow

For Mom and Dad
Preparing our Hearts

Scripture: 1 Thessalonians 5:12-22; Luke 9:23

When I was a teenager there was a Christian song out that talked about even if there were no heaven, I would still follow God. That really struck me. I asked myself if I was following Jesus because I wanted to go to heaven or if I was truly following him because I wanted a relationship with him. I'd been a Christian since I was seven, but during those teenage years, my faith was growing, and I was gaining a deeper understanding of what it meant to follow Christ. When I settled in my heart and mind that I wanted to follow Jesus no matter what, and knowing him was worth everything, I felt such joy and freedom. It was an important moment in my walk with God.

Following Christ challenges us where we struggle the most. The rich man needed to give up his riches (Matthew 19:21-24). The faithful son needed to leave his father (Matthew 8:21-23). The fishermen left their fishing nets (Luke 5:11). Following Christ is wonderful, but it requires sacrifice, recognizing we are not our own, but we are his, and we choose to follow his leading, not our own plans.

Is God asking you to give up something to follow him?

Prayer: Spend some time praying about anything that may be standing in the way of you completely following Christ and pray about anything that is difficult for you to surrender to God.

Preparing to Parent

The main thing we need to make clear with this lesson and others about faith in Christ is helping our children realize they must choose for themselves to follow Christ. They aren't Christians simply because we are. It's not something we can choose for them. We can't force them to follow Jesus. They must make that commitment for themselves. Jesus knows them, loves them, and has a plan for their lives individually and within our family and his church.

They need to come to a point where they understand they need a savior. We can't make that happen, and we shouldn't try to by scaring them with talks about hell. No child wants to go to hell, but not all children know what it means to repent for their own sin. If we push or scare them, they may think they are safe and are saved when they don't really understand.

We do better if we wait for them to begin asking questions. We can teach them about Jesus from day one, but we must allow God to draw them to himself.

For the Family
Enjoying the Lesson Together

Scripture: 1 Thessalonians 5:12-22; Luke 9:23
(remember to choose a verse as your family memory verse with each lesson)

Object Lesson: Follow the Leader Challenge

This is just like any follow-the-leader game except, if you can, make some of the steps or actions difficult for your children where they may ask for your help in following you. Do silly things, hard things, and even stop suddenly and see how they do in stopping too. All of these actions will then be talked about with the verses. How well do we follow Christ? When he says "wait" do we wait well, or do we bump into him or get impatient in waiting? Do we ask for his help and need his help in some of the ways he wants us to follow him?

1 Thessalonians lists so many actions that show we are Christ's followers. Go through the list of things in the verses of things that we are told to do. Can you think of additional things God has told us to do if we want to obediently follow him?

Prayer/Song/Poem: Sing "I Have Decided to Follow Jesus"

Activity: Walk with Each Child

If possible, make time to take a walk with each child alone. During this walk, talk about following Jesus and what that means. Encourage your child to share their ideas and how they understand Jesus. Talk about how following Jesus also means walking alongside him and going where he leads, just like you are leading right now. Discuss how you talk with Jesus along the way as you walk with him.

When you return from your walk, have each child either make a sign of what it means to follow Jesus or write what it means. This can also be done by one child while you're walking with another. For the youngest children, they can draw a picture of following Jesus.

Picture Books: *Go and Do Likewise* by John Hendrix, *Come with Me* by Holly M. McGhee, *Faithful Feet* by Laura Sassi

Read

For Mom & Dad
Preparing Our Hearts

Scripture: Psalm 119

My mom's best friend gave me my first Bible for my eighth birthday after I became a Christian. I was so excited. I took it to my room and started reading. It was a King James Bible, and I didn't understand much of anything I read. I was so upset. So, I prayed. I asked God to help me understand. The next day when I read my Bible, it made sense. I could understand! I was ecstatic. Not only did I understand, but God had answered my prayer. It was a defining moment for me in my walk with God as a young believer.

A recent study shows that reading or interacting with scripture four times a week has a profound effect on our lives. For instance, we are over 200% more likely to tell others about Christ when we encounter the Bible at least four times a week. The study's "research has demonstrated, those who read the Bible at least four times a week are less likely to engage in behaviors such as gambling, pornography, getting drunk, and sex outside marriage." Daily is best, but if we engage in Bible study at least four times each week, we can know that it will truly have a positive effect on our lives and in our families ("Scientific Evidence for the Power of 4," Center for Bible Engagement, December 2009).

However, before we talk about how to make encountering Scripture each week a habit, we need to deal with the elephant in the room. In our Christian Walk, it seems, little causes more guilt in our lives than feeling like a failure in reading our Bibles. We've been told we need to read the Bible daily if we are a good Christian (I could spend a lot of time on that description alone, but let's move on). The need-to-know God's word is paramount in knowing God and how to follow Him. Otherwise, we might be deceived by false teachers. This is a real issue seen throughout history and in our world today as heresies creep into the Church. However, living with the constant sense of failure can damage our walk with God and our relationship with Him almost as much as sins we commit. The main reason is guilt keeps us from fellowshipping with God. We can feel afraid to even approach God with our concerns, needs, or sins because we have failed Him so much. So, what happens? Our Christian Walk becomes a legalistic pattern of trying and failing because we are acting on guilt, living in our own strength, and spend little time in fellowship with God being led by the Holy Spirit. The truth is, our strength as Christ followers comes from our joy in the Lord, not in being determined to be perfect little Christians.

Can we just take a deep breath and relax for a moment? Can we step back and think about the woman caught in adultery? Jesus asked her, "Where are your accusers?" I think Jesus is asking us the same thing. Who is the Accuser? According to Scripture, our Accuser is Satan (Job 1:6, Job 2:1, Zechariah 3:1; Revelation 12:10). Satan and our own perfectionism are our biggest enemies in our walk with God.

So, let's tackle this guilt before we move on. If we are in bondage to guilt, our children will pick that up like picking up a toy off the floor. That's not meant to give you more guilt, but I want us to recognize what the Enemy is trying to do. He wants to hinder our relationship with God and keep our children from God. One of his most effective tools is our bondage to guilt. We'll talk more about guilt in general later. For now, let's look at our guilt over not consistently reading our Bibles.

1. God never said, "Thou shalt read thy Bible daily or else." But we sometimes live like He did. God is not the one convicting us of sin here. Satan is accusing us.
2. God is not expecting our children to be perfect any more than we are expecting that. We know our children are imperfect messes just like we are. And we adore them anyway. Guess what — God, our perfect heavenly Father, looks at us with even more love than we do with our own children.
3. Perfectionism is sin, and it should be confessed and brought to God. He is building a perfect heart within us as we grow more and more Christlike in our walk with God. Perfectionism is us playing God and trying to become perfect in our strength. It falls short of God's perfect will just like every other sin (Romans 3:23).
4. Ideally, yes, we want to read or listen to the Bible daily, even if it is only one verse, to keep our hearts and minds focused on God and to get His word into our hearts; however, that is our ideal and a habit we can build easily when we are not bound up in guilt and attaching this practice to our worth as a child of God. He wants us to know His word, but not out of obligation and fear, but because we love him and want to follow Christ (John 8:31-32).

5. Living the Christian life is not a competition trying to win God's favor. God is not going to love you more than He loves me because you read your Bible more, tell more people about Jesus, or give more money to the church. He already loves you and me with His whole heart.
6. Reading the Bible is a privilege of the modern age. We are so blessed to have the Bible available to us. Not only was it not readily available to individuals in the past, but the early Catholic church also believed it was a sin for the average person to read the Bible.

So, I hope that helps us get a better perspective on Bible reading. Now, how can we joyfully build this habit into our walk with God? In today's family lesson, we talk about several ways, so I won't list them here. However, I do want to encourage you that "reading our Bible" does not mean taking three hours, highlighters in hand, to study the Bible every day. We have times in our lives where we might find a few minutes as we drive to pick up our kids from some activity to listen to the audio Bible. Sometimes, if our children are really young, and we're home taking care of them all day, we can find even that to be a real challenge because when they nap, we clean. When they go to bed, we fall asleep before we can finish a conversation with our spouse. These are temporary but challenging times, and we certainly don't need the added guilt of feeling like a failure over not reading our Bibles enough.

Reading the Bible is different than studying the Bible. Sitting down to do a deep dive into Scripture is awesome, but that is not usually a realistic daily goal. Reading the Bible means listening to it on audio, reading a few verses, or maybe following a reading plan. The habit of reading God's word helps it get into our hearts and minds. Every time we hear it, read it, or study it, it is like God's word comes to life more and more. It gets planted deeper and deeper in our lives.

The writers of the Bible loved the Word of God. They recognized that it nourished them, strengthened them, and guided them. These are the Words of God to us. Many times, people want to know God's will for their lives. Most of it is right there in the Bible. As we grow in our relationship with Him, we grow in godly character, and other small choices needing discernment come into focus. First, we seek to be godly and Christlike in our lives, in our thinking, and in our understanding. Then, the rest, such as what college to attend, what job we should accept, or who to marry, fall into place. God knows our hearts. If they are right with Him, we can follow Him, and even if we miss something or make a mistake, we have the confidence from His Word to know that He will use every mistake in our lives to teach us and grow us. Nothing is wasted with God.

If you are struggling with loving the Word of God, ask God to help you to long for it, to thirst for it. He will answer that prayer.

If you are struggling with reading the Bible, maybe you need a different reading plan. I have a hard time reading most reading plans that take us through Old Testament, New Testament, Psalms, and Proverbs each day. I prefer to go book by book. I remember it better and enjoy it more. I really enjoy reading a chronological Bible reading plan. Seek out what works best for you. You can find many plans on Bible apps like YouVersion. You can add a friend or your family member to read along with you and to leave comments each day on your readings. This allows you to find the kind of reading plan you enjoy, have built-in accountability, and share with and encourage one another while applying what you've read.

Today, for your Bible reading, we look at Psalm 119, the longest chapter in the Bible. It is so beautiful in talking about the Word of God. Spending time meditating on this chapter reminds us why God's Word is so wonderful. Read what you can of it to prepare your hearts for guiding your children.

You may want to worship and pray listening to a song like:
"Your Words Are Wonderful" by Sovereign Grace Music

> *Reverence for the LORD is pure, lasting forever.*
> *The laws of the LORD are true; each one is fair.*
> *They are more desirable than gold, even the finest gold.*
> *They are sweeter than honey, even honey dripping from the comb.*
> *(Psalm 19:9-10, NLT)*

Pray: Pray for an unending thirst for God's Word. Pray for God's Word to come alive for you and your children.

Preparing to Parent

Our children will make Bible reading a priority if we do. Reading God's Word and letting our children see us reading God's Word is important. As parents, we set the example for our kids. Are we reading the Bible and praying often? Do they see us, or do we only read when we're alone in our room?

We can help them see us turn to God's Word often by:
Reading Scripture together at the breakfast table each day.

Quoting a verse that you've memorized together when it fits your situation.
Attending church/Bible study regularly.
Listening to the Bible.

Praying with your children when they have a problem and then asking what Scripture comes to mind or what verses they like to read at that moment to comfort them. If they can't think of one, have one ready to share.

John Wesley's mother used to pray in her chair with her apron over her head. The children knew not to bother her during those times. We tend to want to have our time alone with God, and often we are uncomfortable having others hear us pray aloud. However, when we are parenting, this is vital. Our children need to see us worshipping, praying, and reading the Bible. They need to hear our prayers. When we become comfortable with these activities, they will be comfortable with them too, and they will understand that these are priorities in our lives. They will grasp the importance and know they can find comfort, guidance, and hope in God's Word.

Plan: How will you interact with the Bible this week? How will you make sure your children encounter God's Word? Plan at least four times your family is in God's Word each week (Some examples: Church Sunday morning, Sunday School, weekly small group Bible study, daily verse at breakfast, sticky note with a Bible verse on it stuck to the bathroom mirror, hanging God's word on your wall and reading it together as a family, reading a few verses after reading the bedtime story).

For the Family
Enjoying the Lesson Together

Scripture: 2 Timothy 3:16-17; Psalm 119:9-18
(remember to choose a verse as your family memory verse with each lesson)

Object Lesson: Names for the Bible

Collect these items if you can. Otherwise, use the pictures in this lesson. Put the objects or pictures in the middle of the table. (gold, honey, sword, milk, lamp, flashlight, matches or lighter, hammer, and hard candies or tootsie pops—I like tootsie pops because after they suck on them awhile, they find the chocolatey center—if we meditate on God's Word awhile, soon we seem to gain more understanding and know God more)

Any idea what all these things have in common?

Hint: Our word for today is READ. As Christians, what do we read?

Each of these is used to describe God's word.

(If your kids can read, assign a scripture to each child and have them pick up the object that matches their verse(s) as they read them aloud. Then discuss why and how these describe God's Word).

Gold and Honey: Psalm 19:7-11 — God's word is valuable and sweet to our souls/hearts.
Sword: Heb. 4:12-13; Eph. 6:17 — the Word protects us from Satan's lies, it helps us understand why we choose to do wrong things.
Milk: 1 Peter 2:2 — we need it to grow as a Christian like a baby needs milk
Lamp/flashlight: Ps. 119:105 — it shows us how to walk, following Jesus
Matches or lighter (fire) and a Hammer: Jer. 23:28-29 — God's word reveals the truth so if someone is lying about God, we'll know because God's word burns away the lies and smashes the lies like a hammer.

- *Why is the Bible called the Word of God?*
- *What other "doing" words come to mind about the Word of God? (memorize, meditate, listen, teach, hide it in our hearts, obey, think about) — go over what each word means, and be sure to clarify "meditate" in the Christian understanding distinguishing it from the Eastern type of meditation (Christians fill our minds with God's word and think about what it means, like sucking on a hard candy. However, Eastern meditation says to empty our minds which can open us up to lies and bad thoughts coming in).*
- *Why is God's Word so important for us?*

We're going to practice reading God's Word, talking about what it means, and then meditating on it.

Choose one of the above scriptures. I think Psalm 119:9-18 is better for little kids.

God's word helps us stay pure, have clean hearts, and be right with God when we obey it.

When we hide God's word in our hearts, it means that we put it there like a treasure in a treasure chest, and He can help us remember those words that guide us to make good choices and to follow God's way. They also remind us, when we do make wrong choices, that God still loves us and will forgive us. However, we need to ask for God's forgiveness showing that we are turning away from our sin and following him. God's word is a gift to us and helps us in so many ways.

How do you feel about God's word? Are you like the writer in verses 15-16? Do you feel the same way?

Read those two verses aloud together as a commitment and prayer to God and add verses 17-18.

Prayer/Song/Poem: If you know Amy Grant's song "Thy Word," teach it to your kids, even if you just teach the chorus: Thy word is a lamp unto my feet and a light unto my path (repeat)

Or Cedarmont Worship for Kids 2 has a kid-friendly version of Grant's song.

Activity: Learning to Look Up Verses or Bible Drill

If your children are not familiar with how to look up a verse, show them how to find a book, the chapter, and verse.

Put a drop of honey on the tongue of each child and read Psalm 19:9-10 together. Use these verses to help children learn how to look up a verse.

Then have a Bible drill practicing looking up verses. Work in teams if you have very young children.

Matthew 6:23, John 3:16, Genesis 1:1, Proverbs 17:17, Romans 10:9-10, Psalm 23:1, Philippians 1:6, Psalm 139:14, Ephesians 6:1, Colossians 3:20

Learn a song for the books of the Bible: Mary Rice Hopkins has one, and there are several others.

Picture Books: *Read It, See It, Sing It: Knowing and Loving the Bible* by Hunter Beless; *God Speaks to Me (For the Bible Tells Me So series)* by Kristen Wetherell, *Where Is Wisdom* by Scott James

54

Memorize

For Mom & Dad
Preparing Our Hearts

Scripture: John 17:13-21

    I've been memorizing scripture most of my life, but when I was a young bride, it really made a huge difference in my life. My husband had cancer, and I became consumed with fear. The doctor said if we hadn't caught it when we did, Dave would have been dead within a month. Hearing that, I didn't think of how miraculously God had spared his life, but rather how quickly I could have lost him. As fear began to rule my thoughts each day, I decided to go to a counselor. The first thing he had me do was memorize 2 Timothy 1:7, and we would say that verse each time we met. It began to break down the stronghold of fear and rebuild a firm foundation of faith. When I read the verses that say God's word is powerful, I know it is true. His word made all the difference in my life.

    As we talk about memorizing Scripture, John 17 reminds us why we do it, in a beautiful prayer from the heart of Jesus for all of us. Focus on verses 13-21. I especially love reading it in the Amplified version of the Bible.

    Jesus says that He has given us God's word (v. 14). His word helps make us holy, set apart, for God's work. We also understand spiritual things because of His word and His Spirit in our lives. The world does not understand this, and so it hates us (1 Cor. 2:14).

    Then He talks about keeping us safe and sanctifying us in the truth from His word.

    Equipped with His Word, sanctified, strengthened, and protected by His Word, we are being sent into the world to tell others about all He has taught us (Matthew 28:19-20). And it begins with our children.

Finally, I love verses 20-21 where Jesus literally prays for us. So much of the Bible is written specifically to people of that day but applies to us. This is a place where Jesus specifically prays for us. Isn't it wonderful?

We don't memorize Scripture out of a sense of duty or obligation. It's not meant to be a chore. We memorize it because we need it. It nourishes us and strengthens us. It protects and guides us. And it reveals the heart of God toward us. Scripture reminds us that we serve an awesome, loving Father worthy of all our praise.

Your testimonies are my heritage forever,
for they are the joy of my heart.
(Psalm 119:111, ESV)

Prayer: Ask God to help you successfully hide His Word in your heart in creative ways; like with reading Scripture, if you find you don't have a desire to memorize God's Word.

Scripture: Psalm 119:11; Psalm 1:1-3; Colossians 3:16; Deuteronomy 11:18
(remember to choose a verse as your family memory verse with each lesson)

Preparing to Parent
Kids have amazing brains and can memorize much easier than we can. One of our main jobs at this point is to be careful what we say about memorization. If we act frustrated or talk constantly about how we can't memorize, our children very likely will pick up that negative attitude about memorizing. If we remember when we were children, we probably remember enjoying memorizing. We learned songs, chants, grammar rules I rhyme, and all our math facts. We were like sponges. How wonderful to help our children become sponges of God's word.

I heard a pastor say the other day, "Don't tell me you can't memorize things. When you leave here today, are you going to your home? Do you know how to get there? Then you can memorize things." So true. We memorize information constantly. But we do it without thinking about it or worrying about it. We don't usually think about laboring over it. What if we approached Bible memory with the same attitude? That same pastor said if we give ourselves four minutes a day, we can memorize a portion of scripture each week. He suggests something like this type of schedule:

Sunday: Read through the whole passage you plan to memorize for four minutes.

Monday: Read through the whole passage three times and fill the rest of the four minutes trying to say it from memory.

Tuesday: Read through the whole passage twice, then try to say it from memory totaling four minutes.

Wednesday: Read through the passage once, then spend the rest of the 4 minutes trying to say it from memory.

Thursday: Spend four minutes quoting the verses.

Friday: Write down the verses and recite them from memory for four minutes.

Saturday: Spend four minutes reciting the passage from memory.

I would add, pray daily for God to give you a spirit of delight and joy in memorizing Scripture. Ask that He makes this a fun and joyful time with your children.

For the Family
Enjoying the Lesson Together

Object Lesson: Creative Bible Memory

"Today we are going to think of creative ways to memorize Bible verses."

1. Choose your verse you want to practice. I recommend Psalm 119:11 for demonstration.
2. "Starting with brushing our teeth, we will read and think the verse in our minds. While we wash our hands we will say it. While we brush our hair we will say it."
3. Then, go outside and bounce a ball and say it again.
4. March around the living room and say it.
5. If you can find a song, sing it. Steve Green has this in a song. Proclaim Ministries has a video showing hand motions for learning the verse.
6. If you know ASL or want to learn it, saying the verse in sign language can really help us learn it quickly. YouTube has many videos that can help.

Say something like: "The Bible tells us we should memorize and meditate on God's word. What does meditate mean?

We can also memorize by playing games. Let's try one. I'll say the first word, and we'll go around the table each saying one word until we've said the whole verse."

What does it mean to hide God's Word in our hearts?

Why would we do that?

Sometimes we hide something because we don't want someone to steal it. Who would try to steal God's word from our hearts?

We want to keep God's word in our hearts, so He can remind us of it when we need it:
To help us think right and remember God is with us.
To give us God's wisdom.
To have His strength when facing temptations.
To help us make right choices and to know how God wants us to live.

Prayer/Song/Poem: Sing the Bible verse song again and pray asking God to help us learn His Word and hide it in our hearts.

Activity: Choose verse(s) to memorize.

Write out the verse.

Do one of the movement activities to learn it.

Using a white board or chalk board, write out the verse with the reference/address first, then the verse, and then the reference/address again.

Say it together, then erase a word.

Say it again together. Then erase another word.

Say it again together. Now erase one or two more words.

Keep saying it until all the words are erased, and you can say it from memory.

If your family is musical, you may want to make up a song for your verse(s).

Hang the verses each child wrote out on the wall of their bedroom or on their bedroom door. Put a sticky note of it on the mirror in the bathroom so everyone can review it this week.

Start making a plan to memorize a verse or two each week (I have a free program on social media called 2 in 7 where we offer two verses to memorize each week. You can find it if you link to my Facebook or Instagram accounts from my website: TerrieHellardBrown.com)

Picture Books: *Strong: Psalm 1* by Sally Lloyd Jones (she has several books about scripture depending on what you decide to memorize, you may want to choose one of the others). *Nothing* by Natalee Creech, *Where Is Wisdom?* by Scott James

Pray (How to Pray)

For Mom & Dad
Preparing Our Hearts

Scripture: Mark 12:30-31; Psalm 55:17; 1 Thessalonians 5:16-18

The early days of parenting are so scary at times. We question ourselves, and when a child is ill, we hope we are doing what's right. My three older children and my husband all got chicken pox. I had them when I was in first grade, so I was immune. I remember what it was like even now. So, I knew what to expect with my kids, I thought. However, after my youngest was doing fine and my husband was on the mend, my older son and daughter were still having a hard time. It seemed the virus had gotten into my daughter's joints, and she was having trouble walking. However, that resolved rather quickly, and she was getting well. My son, however, just didn't seem to be getting well. I prayed, and I felt strongly that I needed to call the doctor. They had me bring him into the hospital, and we learned he had a secondary dangerous staph infection. They told me if we hadn't brought him in, he probably would have died. As terrifying as that was to hear, I was so thankful that God had spoken to my heart during prayer.

We know praying each day for our children is an important part of being a parent, and occasionally it's important to pray for them many times during the day. Sometimes we agonize over our children and the hard things they deal with or the bad choices they've made.

One of the ways I like to pray for my kids is to think through the greatest commandment because it covers every part of our lives. When I think through it for each child, I think of the various areas of their lives and what they need prayer for in those areas. We can pray this way for our spouse and others especially when we're not sure what they might need us to pray for. I use Mark's version because he includes the strength part.

> "And you shall love the Lord your God with all your *heart* and
> with all your *soul* and with all your *mind* and with all your *strength*.'
> The second is this: 'You shall love your *neighbor* as yourself.'
> There is no other commandment greater than these."
> (Mark 12:30-31, ESV)

Heart: What's going on in this child's emotional life? Where are they struggling? Pray for emotional intelligence and maturity, that this child can master any anger, anxiety, or overwhelming emotions. Pray for peace and joy to fill this child's life. Pray for protection from the enemy who wants to steal, kill, and destroy, including your child's innocence. Your prayers can help guard this child's heart.

Soul: Where is this child spiritually? What temptations and struggles need prayer? Pray for this child's salvation and faithfulness to God. Pray that this child will answer God's call in life and be a committed member at church. Pray the Truth would be revealed to them, their mind renewed, and their desires turned toward God.

Mind: What does this child need prayer for regarding education, thought patterns, and distractions? Does this child have learning disabilities or delays you can pray for? Pray for academic success. Pray for mental health. Pray for this child's creativity. Pray protection over this child's mind and thoughts as well as dreams at night. Pray for protection from all the ideas thrown at this child at school, with friends, on television, or other devices.

Strength: What physical needs does this child have? Pray for health and strength. Pray for protection from injury, physical abuse, and unhealthy choices. Pray that this child will desire good and healthy food, activities, and relationships. Pray for exercise and a love for hard work.

Neighbor or Social Life: Pray for this child to make wise choices when choosing friends. Pray for healthy socialization, strong relationship skills, and friendliness. Pray for this child to find a place in the social structure we're living in, and for this child to dream of a future career and goals. Pray that this child will show mercy and grace to others and find forgiveness for others. Pray this child is trustworthy and kind. Pray for this child's future spouse. Pray that this child finds favor with God and man. Pray that if living for Christ means going against culture, that this child will be strong and courageous.

As you pray through these five areas for each child, of course, you will add your specific requests for each one.

Preparing to Parent

One of the hardest parts of discipling our children is seeing how they process and understand what we share with them. What undertones do they feel or what misunderstandings might they have? It is necessary to check for understanding frequently and let the children express their feelings and questions.

For example, parents might teach about praying for others and to lead with prayers for others first. One child joyfully participates, praying often and enjoying the activities. Another carries a burden of feeling he can never pray for himself because he must always put others first. He must focus on God and others keeping himself last to the point that he begins to feel resentful.

As our children grow, we might face what a friend of mine dealt with in teaching her daughters to dress modestly. She had learned to be modest as a child and wanted her daughters to respect their bodies and dress modestly too. However, one of her daughters internalized this to mean her body was wicked, and she was evil. She began to loathe her own body. She became afraid of men because she felt they were always thinking lustful things about women. She even decided she was gay and eventually deconstructed her faith.

Checking for understanding and listening to how our children are processing the lessons we're teaching and the guidance we're giving may be key to helping our children find and hold on to God and Truth. We may be able to eliminate misunderstandings that may bring harm or cause a dysfunctional faith.

As our children get older, we must choose our battles wisely. This is a tough one, but maybe we let our daughter know why we don't think she should be on the worship team with her midriff showing. Hopefully, knowing the why will help kids make a better choice on their own.

When a child is overwhelmed by constantly praying for others and a fear about praying for himself, we can model different types of prayer. We can talk about urgent prayer where we stop and pray for the request without going through a whole prayer even if the request is for ourselves (I use the example of when we are getting ready for a test in class, we don't pray a big long prayer, we pray a quick "Help me, Lord" prayer and start on the test), and devotional or extended prayer when we spend time praising, thanking, confessing, and worshiping before we pray for the requests. We can do circle prayer time where we ask each person what their requests/needs are. Then we pray for that person before moving to the next person.

Another way we can model prayer is by showing how, when someone comes with a request (such as a child who had a nightmare or a church friend after the worship service who comes up and asks for prayer), we stop immediately and pray for that person. We don't make it a big prayer beginning with praise and worship. We just get right to the need.

After modeling praying in urgent situations, when we teach the five-finger prayer or the PRAY acrostic, the child understands that it is a model of prayer to use in our quiet time or extended prayer times. They can see that prayer is not a formula or a legalistic practice but spending time talking with our Heavenly Father just like we might spend time talking with our dad.

For the Family
Enjoying the Lesson Together

Scripture: Psalm 55:17; 1 Thessalonians 5:16-18
    (remember to choose a verse as your family memory verse with each lesson)

We have three lessons on prayer. I hope these lessons help you find fun and creative ways to help your children fall in love with prayer and strengthen their faith in the God who always hears.

Object Lesson: PRAY Action Chant

One of our goals is to help our children learn that they can pray anytime, anywhere, and that we are told to pray continuously.

The object lesson is their own hands and bodies and ways to remember how to pray.

What is prayer?
Why do we pray?
We can use PRAY to remind us to pray different ways.

P = praise (raise your hands up as you praise God—even lying in bed)
  When we pray, we should praise and worship God, thanking Him for all He's done and for who He is.

R = repent (put your hands over your heart and bow your head)
  We need to repent of our sins. That means to confess what we've done wrong and turn away from it. We want to follow Jesus and walk away from sin.

A = ask (put your hands together in front of you like a traditional prayer icon, then go through the five-finger prayer reminder—see below)
  In prayer we can ask God anything. We can ask Him for wisdom, help, protection, healing and for anything we need. We can ask Him for what we want. We know He will answer us with the best answer. He won't give us something we shouldn't have. He knows what is best for us always.

Y=yield (stretch your arms wide in surrender to God)

Yield means to choose to follow God's plan instead of our own. It means I will give up or yield my own desires so I can follow God's will for my life. As we pray, sometimes God's Spirit will put something on our hearts or in our minds that we need to do or change. When we respond with "yes, Lord" we are yielding to God.

When we think of asking in prayer, how can we remember what to ask or who to pray for? One way is the five-finger prayer.

Put your hands together like you are going to pray. Closest to you are your thumbs. This reminds us to pray for those closest to us like our family, grandparents, and friends.

Next are our pointer fingers. Who are the people who point you in the right direction? For example: Teachers, Pastors, Sunday School Teacher.

Next are our middle fingers, and they are our tallest or longest fingers. They remind us to pray for those who are over us like the President, police officers and other community helpers, and our school principal and those who lead the school board.

Then, we see our ring fingers. Those are our weakest fingers on our hands, so they remind us to pray for those who are weakest around us. Maybe we want to pray for the poor, the homeless, the sick, or others who are weak and struggling in some way.

Finally, we have our pinky fingers, our last fingers. This reminds us that Jesus wants us to also pray for ourselves, but it is good to wait until last to pray for ourselves. We should be humble, gentle, and patient as followers of Christ, and praying for ourselves last helps us remember that when we are doing our prayer time each day.

Let your children know they do not have to put their hands up, and they don't even have to pray for themselves last every time, but these are ways to remind us how to pray, not a formula. Sometimes, we are scared, and we just cry out to God for help. Sometimes we pray for God to help us remember what we've studied before we take a test. Sometimes we know someone is hurting, and we just pray for that person. The Bible tells us to pray continually. So, we pray wherever we are, about whatever is on our hearts at the moment, but we should set aside time to pray through our prayer reminders each day too—maybe when we've read our Bibles and are focusing on God each morning or evening.

Remember Psalm 55:17 and try to do a full prayer each day.

Prayer/Song/Poem: To end today, pray sentence prayers (where each person takes turns praying a one-sentence prayer.) Go through the PRAY acrostic and have each person pray one sentence for each part before moving to the next part. Everyone will start by praying something to praise and thank God. Then, go around the circle to repent and ask for God's mercy and forgiveness. Each person can ask for one thing in a one-sentence prayer, and end with everyone praying about an area where they need to trust God more. You may need to guide younger children or have them repeat a prayer after you when you first begin teaching them to pray.

Activities: Read a book together

Because this lesson is at bedtime, the only activity you may want to add is reading a book together and ending with prayer.

Picture Books: *Any Time Any Place Any Prayer* by Laura Wifler, *In Jesus' Name I Pray* by Costi and Christine Hinn (Three books for parents: *Prayer* by O. Hallesby, *Anything* by Jennie Allen, and *Prayer Saturated Family* by Cheryl Sacks)

Pray (Lord's Prayer and Prayer Walks)

For Mom & Dad
Preparing Our Hearts

Scripture: Psalm 143:1; James 5:16

One of my favorite memories of serving in Taiwan was prayer walking around the island during several mission trips. What made it so wonderful was our children being there with us and taking part. Now, almost 20 years later, they still talk about those memories. They are their favorite ones as well. What amazes me is that we didn't always see the results of those prayers. However, we all knew God was working. We could sense his presence. So often we think of answered prayer as showing us how powerful God is, but we can also experience God's power and presence simply as we do what we are called to do. Seeing my kids' responses to these experiences back then encouraged me so much that they were growing in their relationship with God.

As our children get older, they need to make their faith their own. They cannot just follow in our footsteps and use our faith alone. Part of that process means that we may run into some situations that concern us or even frighten us. Our kids, as they become adults, make decisions we may not agree with. It can be difficult, but the above verses give us comfort and guidance.

No matter how hopeless situations may seem, we must continue to pray. God is at work. God hears our prayers, and he knows our hearts. He can bring healing in the most troublesome of circumstances. I've repeatedly witnessed God answer the prayers of parents for their children and children for their parents. God is good. We just need to pray and trust God with those we love.

Scripture: Matthew 6:9-13 (Memorizing these scriptures may be a goal you have for your children/for your family. Because they've heard it before, most likely, it is easy to memorize the whole prayer).

Preparing to Parent: The Lord's Prayer or Model Prayer is a common section of scripture most Christians and even non-Christians know. Our children can memorize this easily, and they will know it quickly. However, we want to make sure they understand what they've memorized. Working on understanding helps them use the same ideas as they create their own prayers.

Some churches have books of prayer, and you can also find books with prayers for children to memorize. We don't need to shy away from prayer books, but we can teach our children to add their own prayers to what they memorize. The key to making them meaningful is helping our children use these memorized prayers to guide them as they create their own prayers, or instead, they may want to add their own prayers at the end of memorized prayers.

Prayer Walking is another effective and meaningful way to pray. Below is an article we've often used in preparing our church group to prayer walk (your activity for this dinner time lesson). We don't know who wrote it, so we aren't able to give credit for that. It was given to us in a training we attended many years ago by a missionary. You can also find books written about prayer walking if you want to learn more such as *Prayer Walking: Praying on Site with Insight* by Steve Hawthorne and Graham Kendrick. I believe the missionary may have adapted her talk from this book.

Prayer Walking

14 Are any of you sick? You should call for the elders of the church to come and pray over you, anointing you with oil in the name of the Lord. 15 Such a prayer offered in faith will heal the sick, and the Lord will make you well. And if you have committed any sins, you will be forgiven. 16 Confess your sins to each other and pray for each other so that you may be healed. The earnest prayer of a righteous person has great power and produces wonderful results. 17 Elijah was as human as we are, and yet when he prayed earnestly that no rain would fall, none fell for three and a half years! 18 Then, when he prayed again, the sky sent down rain and the earth began to yield its crops. (James 5:14-18, NLT)

1. Prayer walking is something we plan occasionally. It is not usually a daily prayer practice unless a family decides to include it as part of a family's daily walk through their neighborhood.
2. Prayer walking is **"praying on site with insight."**: As we intercede for those in our neighborhoods, we allow the Spirit to guide us in how to pray on the spot. You may be led by God to bless a home you pass or to intercede for someone held in spiritual bondage. You will begin to sense what needs are in your area.
3. Prayer walking is **quietly interceding** for the people we walk past everyday: It is not a noisy parade or a demonstration. Even if you pray out loud as you walk, it should remain unobtrusive.
4. Prayer walking can be done with a friend using **conversational prayer**: As you walk and talk, you are simply voicing your prayer to each other and to God like you're having a conversation as He walks along with you too.
5. Prayer walking is **spiritual warfare**: As you walk, you may become aware of dark influences or strongholds. You are on the frontlines of spiritual warfare and need to be prepared. We do not fear evil, but we need to be ready to battle it as we encounter it.
6. Prayer walking **opens doors**: People may come up to you and ask you questions. Or you may feel that you should ask someone on the street how you can pray for them today.
7. Prayer walking is praying with your **eyes open** (literally and spiritually): We walk with our eyes open because it can be painful to walk down the street with them closed! ☺ But we walk with our spiritual eyes open to the Spirit's leading and insight.

    If we all commit to this kind of prayer, we can also use it during other walking times, not just when a prayer walk event is planned. We can **blanket our city with prayer daily** as we walk to exercise, walk our dogs, or walk on our way somewhere.

Some simple pointers:
1. Be alert as you walk. Safety first! (We can learn from Pokemon Go players who have been injured while walking by watching their phone screens rather than their surroundings and pay attention as you walk).
2. Feel free to pray either silently or aloud. And don't let moments of silence make you or your prayer partner(s) feel uncomfortable.

3. Be aware of how the Holy Spirit may be leading. He may, for example, prompt you to speak to someone along the way to invite him or her to church. If He does, enjoy the opportunity to be His gentle voice of encouragement. You might be the only smile that person gets all day!

4. Bring a pen and notebook (or your Smartphone notepad), just in case you want to make a personal notation about a place or person or insight the Lord gives you.

5. Share your experience with others. Your faith will be strengthened, and you will also encourage others.

6. Don't stop after just one walk! Watch God continue His work around you as you make praying for your community a regular and consistent part of your life. The blessings will be yours!

For the Family
Enjoying the Lesson Together

At Dinner: Lord's Prayer

Let's look at a prayer Jesus used to model how we should pray. We call it the Lord's Prayer, but it is not something we are supposed to just memorize and repeat. It shows us how to pray.

One of the main parts of this prayer is not in the words as much as in our attitude. Any time we are praying, we need to be humble and worshipful toward God. When we are humble, that means that we focus on God and honor Him with our words and have hearts filled with thankfulness. When we have these attitudes, we worship God as we pray.

Sometimes we may pray in a hurry, especially if we are afraid or someone is hurt. That's okay too, but this prayer shows us how to pray a longer, thoughtful prayer honoring God with our words and attitudes. Jesus taught his disciples to pray this way.

Our Father, who is in heaven,
We address our prayers to God
Hallowed be Your name.

We honor God's name and want others to acknowledge His goodness and holiness; we worship Him.

Your kingdom come.

We pray for God's ways to affect our world—that more people will faithfully follow God so we can see His kingdom here on earth.

Your will be done, on earth as it is in heaven.

We pray for God's will to be done on earth, that His plans will prevail. We ask for God to help us be faithful and help others to be faithful to God's will, plan, and ways.

Give us this day our daily bread.

After we honor God and pray for his will, we shift to praying for our needs.

And forgive us our debts, as we also have forgiven our debtors.

We must forgive others so that God can forgive us. (See Matthew 18.) We desperately need His forgiveness because we fail often.

And do not lead us into temptation, but deliver us from evil.

God doesn't tempt us in the sense that He doesn't tempt us to sin. Even when we are tempted, He provides a way out (1 Cor. 10:13) if we will just take it. This, in the original language meant more like we're asking God not to test our faith too much. And that He protect us from evil and temptation. That He would deliver us from the devil's snares if we do stumble.

For Yours is the kingdom and the power and the glory forever. Amen

We end with worship again. Older manuscripts did not have this line, but we often pray it, and it is a good thing to begin and end a prayer with worship and honoring God. We can't do that enough.

(Matthew 6:9-13, NASB)

Prayer/Song/Poem: YouTube has several versions of "The Lord's Prayer" songs for kids to help with memorizing and learning to say the prayer.

Activities: Prayer Walk

Another amazing way we can pray is while walking through a neighborhood. We call this a prayer walk. After dinner tonight, we are going to walk and pray.

Prepare your family beforehand because sometimes God opens conversations with people along the way, and sometimes you might encounter some spiritual warfare which usually, by our experience, results in the children sensing where something is wrong and needs prayer.

While you walk, you pray aloud with your eyes open. You stop and pray when you feel you should, but mostly you pray for the people and places you walk past.

Prayer walking is a wonderful way to involve children in missions as well. When we prayer walk we often start conversations with people and get to know people. Our children are actively a part of ministry and missions as they pray for others and get to know new people. When we prayer walked in Manong in Taiwan, the first day was prayer walking, but the second day our team would go back to the same neighborhoods and hand out books and Bibles especially to children. The children on the team were able to take part in this activity as well.

Picture Books: *Any Time Any Place Any Prayer* by Laura Wifler, *In Jesus' Name I Pray* by Costi and Christine Hinn (Three books for parents: *Prayer* by O. Hallesby, *Anything* by Jennie Allen, and *Prayer Saturated Family* by Cheryl Sacks)

Pray (God Answers)

For Mom & Dad
Preparing Our Hearts

Scripture: Philippians 4:6; Matthew 7:7-11

Many of our prayers as parents are urgent prayers in a moment of possible disaster. My older son gave me a few of those experiences. One was when we moved into a new apartment. Nate was a helpful child, and he dug into one of the boxes in the bedroom. Unfortunately, it was not a bedroom box, but a kitchen box that should not have been in there. He pulled out a huge butcher knife and came walking down the hall saying, "Mommy, danger." I knew one of us was about to be seriously hurt! I prayed one of those panic prayers, and I tried desperately to remain calm as I walked toward him to get the knife. He stopped walking and let me get the knife, and no one was injured. I told him he was right, that it was definitely dangerous. I tried explaining that when he finds something dangerous, he can come get me rather than bringing it to me so that he is safer. But mostly, I thanked God profusely for protecting us.

As parents, we battle worry (and sometimes danger) all the time. Raising little humans is a difficult and challenging adventure. We love them so much and want to make the right choices guiding them correctly toward God and toward being responsible adults. The job can feel daunting.

The best answer to how to walk through this adventure well is prayer. The Bible tells us to bring our concerns to God. If we lack wisdom, to ask God. He not only gave us these children to raise; he equips us and is with us through every step. We can rest in that knowledge and find peace as we parent.

We may have heard others say or said it ourselves: "I can't do anything else but pray." It's like we think prayer is a last resort and something we do when we are completely hopeless and unable to solve the problem ourselves. I want to challenge all of us to change our mindset. Even if we can tackle the problem ourselves and do something to change the situation, our first resort, our first action, should be prayer. It is the best thing we can do. It is the most important thing we can do. O. Hallesby in his book *Prayer* says prayer is a Christian's main occupation. Prayer changes things because God changes things when we pray. He may have chosen to change the situation even if we didn't pray, but when we pray, we become a part of what God is doing in our family, our community, and our world. We also become more aware of his work and ways and are more attuned to hearing his Spirit speak to our hearts.

Preparing to Parent

Prayer is the opposite of worry. Both are contagious practices for our kids. If they see us praying and trusting God, they usually learn to pray and trust God. If they see us worrying, they will most likely learn to worry. If they see us praying and still worrying or trying to solve the problem ourselves, they will usually pick up the same habit and not learn to trust God in prayer. I say this not to shame us, but to alert us.

Hopefully our children are shielded from most of the things we are tempted to worry about, but when they get older, they either notice our concerns or have their own. Even while they are young, we may need to help them face heavy burdens from bullying or shaming or confusing information about gender, God, and violence.

The best way to begin dealing with all of these very serious issues is prayer. Bringing God into the middle of our problems is the best response we can choose. Anything else should be an outgrowth from prayer and the leading of the Holy Spirit.

God is not surprised by these events and cultural issues. He is greater than any of them, and our prayers help us find his peace and guidance through them all. Our children learn how to deal with struggles, challenges, and terrible situations, learning that God is powerful and present in every situation.

For the Family
Enjoying the Lesson Together

Scripture: Matthew 7:7-11; 1 Thessalonians 5:16-18
(remember to choose a verse as your family memory verse with each lesson)

Object Lesson: Rock and Snake

At breakfast, if you can, get a rock and a rubber snake. If you can't get a rock and a rubber snake, think of your own object lesson. What does your child often ask for, and what would be absurd for you to give them instead (they want a hug and you give them a stinky sneaker instead; or they want to play catch and you have them help you mop the floor instead in answer to their heart's cry).

If you want to be dramatic, as one parent is fixing breakfast, put plates in front of each child with a rock and a rubber snake on it and announce that this is their breakfast.

Otherwise, as you're getting ready for breakfast or even while eating breakfast, talk about how God hears every prayer and answers it with what He knows is best. God is a perfect Father who loves His children. Mom is making biscuits (or pancakes/toast/French toast) for breakfast. If you asked me for one of the biscuits, what would happen? Let's try it. (Child asks for a biscuit, put a stone and a biscuit on the table). Which one would I give you as your father? Yes, because I love you, I would never give you a stone when you asked for a biscuit.

If you asked me for some eggs or toast for breakfast, what would I give you? Put the snake and toast or eggs on the table. I wouldn't be a very nice father if I gave you a snake when you asked for eggs and toast, would I? In the same way, when we ask God for something, He hears us, and He answers. He isn't going to give us something bad when we ask for something. However, I have one more example.

If you asked me for candy for breakfast, what would I give you? That's right. Because I love you, I would not give you candy. I want you to be healthy and to feel good as you go into your day. So, I might say no to something you ask for because it isn't what is best for you, but I would not play tricks on you and give you bad things when you ask for good things.

God is that way with us in answering our prayers. He says to ask and keep on asking. He will answer our prayers with yes, no, or wait.

Read Matthew 7:7-11.

Prayer/Song/Poem: Thanksgiving Prayer

We also thank God for all the wonderful things He gives us. At each meal we thank Him for our food. But we also need to thank Him for answered prayer. Spend some time praying a prayer of thanksgiving for the food and God's blessings.

Prayer/Song/Poem: We can pray different ways. We can bow our heads and close our eyes. We can pray while we walk and talk to one another. We can pray silently during class or out loud at the table before meals.

Activities: Prayer Chain

Another way we pray is to pray for the requests others share. Let's share the prayer requests we have and create a prayer chain.

Supplies needed:

construction paper or other colorful paper (you can choose colors that complement the room where you'll hang it, or make it festive and fun)

scissors

pens

mason jar

glue or staples/stapler

magnets or pushpins (for fridge or bulletin board)

Construction:

Make a prayer chain out of construction paper.

To do this, cut strips of construction paper about 8 inches long and 1 ½ inches wide. Stand these in a jar with a pen or two.

Everyone takes a strip and writes down a prayer request then shares his/her request with the family. These strips are put on a bulletin board or fridge so everyone can remember to pray for them.

When a prayer is answered, put the date on it, and then attach it to the chain.

The chain should be hung up high, like over a window, and eventually you'll have a chain of answered prayers around the top of the room like a garland.

Picture Books: *Any Time Any Place Any Prayer* by Laura Wifler, *In Jesus' Name I Pray* by Costi and Christine Hinn (Three books for parents: *Prayer* by O. Hallesby, *Anything* by Jennie Allen, and *Prayer Saturated Family* by Cheryl Sacks)

Thank

For Mom and Dad
Preparing Our Hearts

Scripture: Colossians 3:15-17; Ephesians 5:20

My dad and I have a good relationship now, but for a part of my childhood, we didn't really. He traveled a lot, and I always felt like I never measured up to his expectations. When I was an adult, I found that my thoughts about my dad were more negative than positive, and I knew that didn't honor him or God. Someone suggested I write a list of gratitude to my dad. I started from when I had my earliest memories and went through the years of my life writing a huge thank you note to my dad. I was amazed at how much I had to be thankful for. Rather than focusing on what I felt I missed out on, I found appreciation for him. As I found this new gratitude, I also found healing. It was the beginning of repairing our relationship. Later, God really got hold of my dad's heart, and he is now a different man. But I am so thankful my healing started before then for me. It was so good for me to be able to love, appreciate, and accept my dad before he was changed into this godly man I now know and thank God for.

Thanksgiving is a superpower God has given us. He tells us repeatedly to be thankful and to give thanks. God knows when we are thankful and content with what we have. His grace carries us through life. Rather than focusing on all our wants and dissatisfactions, we find peace and joy as we focus on his many blessings in our lives. Giving thanks changes our thinking and our outlook. It's like walking on a sunny day, and instead of focusing on the hot sidewalk, someone says, "Look up!" and we see the beautiful blue sky filled with fluffy white clouds and feel the soft breeze blowing past our face. We can't help but smile.

In addition, being thankful helps keep our hearts close to God and helps us have the right attitude in life which then helps us share God with the world. We see in Scripture, the times when God was most displeased with his people were when they grumbled and complained. If we are thankful, we aren't grumbling and complaining. We honor God with our lips and with our attitudes when we are grateful. Plus, we show the world that our God is our Provider and Sustainer. They see our joy and peace even in the hard times of life because we are filled with gratitude.

So, today, we need to think on those things that help us focus on all that God has done in our lives, in our families, and all he has provided for us. God is so good. He is generous. He is loving. He is gracious. Let's thank him for all he has done. You may want to write a thank you note to God like I did my dad. The task really opens our eyes to all we have to be grateful for.

Prayer: We can spend time genuinely thanking God for his goodness in our lives. We can ask him to shift our thinking—to renew our minds—so that we focus on him and his provision rather than what we wish we had. God is so good. Let's focus on his goodness.

Some songs you may want to listen to as a part of prayer or worship:
"Counting Every Blessing" by Rend Collective
"I'm So Blessed" by Cain
"Counting My Blessings" by Matt Maher
"Blessings" by Laura Story
"We Give Thanks" by Sovereign Grace Music

Preparing to Parent

As we've said many times, we aren't just trying to raise obedient children who make us look good—although I think we all would like that too. We are really trying to raise responsible adults who love and follow God with all their hearts. A huge part of that is creating thankful children. Without gratitude, we see our children develop an attitude of entitlement and rudeness resulting in them becoming spoiled, ungrateful, selfish people or living in a world of constant unmet expectations and frustration and anger sometimes leading to violence. It's alarming how ingratitude and entitlement can destroy people's lives and even damage society.

Gratitude is one of those things that every single parent needs to be aware of in their children's lives, whether they are Christian or not. But as Christian parents, we really need to help our children see the importance of being thankful. It's a heart condition that shows when our attitudes are in the wrong place.

So, as we prepare to parent, we should pray for discernment and awareness. We need to pray that God shows us when our children are not thankful but are showing signs of entitlement and selfish expectations. We can address the issue more effectively when we are aware of it. We need to pray that God will help our children's hearts to be softened and ready to learn true gratitude, not just words, but heartfelt, genuine, humble thankfulness with God and others.

For the Family
Enjoying the Lesson Together

Scripture: Colossians 3:15-17; Ephesians 5:20; Psalm 100; Hebrews 12:28; 1 Thessalonians 5:18; Psalm 107:1-31
(remember to choose a verse as your family memory verse with each lesson)

Object Lesson: Gratitude Adds

In this lesson you may use small cookies, marbles, M&M's, Skittles, pennies, grapes, or whatever you want that your children will like, but each child needs a bowl or plate of about 10 of whatever that item is. An extra bowl/plate of more of the item should be in the middle of the table.

Each person draws a paper from the jar and reads it. If it is a complaint, they must put one of their items in the bowl in the center of the table. If it is a positive statement, they add to their bowl/plate from the bowl in the center of the table.

After all the papers are read, each person looks to see how many items they have left.

When we complain, it takes away from our joy and happiness. It also takes away from our closeness to God. When we are thankful, it adds joy to our lives and draws us closer to God.

Have each person count their blessings in their bowls. Remind everyone that we need to count our blessings and be thankful.

What if some have fewer blessings than others? We count our own blessings, so we focus on and are grateful for them. We don't focus on others' blessings to feel jealous or upset if they receive more than we do. In addition, we certainly shouldn't gloat or feel proud if we seem more blessed than others. If we focus on someone else's blessings, we do it so we can rejoice with them. Rejoicing with others and focusing on our blessings can be huge in helping our children grow in their abilities to find gratitude.

Prayer/Song/Poem: Have each person share something they are thankful for. Have a parent close in prayer. Have a parent hand out an extra candy or item to each person after the time of prayer.

Enjoy the items if they are food and enjoy some time talking together around the table.

Activity: Thank You Notes and Thank You Jar

You can choose from two activities:

Write a thank you note to someone and one to God.

Start a thank you jar or tree where family members write what they are thankful for, and at the end of a certain amount of time (a month, the end of the year or beginning of the new year), read all the thank yous.

Picture Books: *The Berenstain Bears Count Their Blessings* by Jan and Stan Berenstain, *Those Shoes* by Maribeth Boelts, *Thank You, God!* by Kathleen Bostrom

Write out and cut apart the sentences and put them in a jar by either copying the page or writing them on cardstock or construction paper.

I don't like my history class. It is boring and has too much work.

Math is too hard. I don't like it.

Why do I have to wash the dishes?

Can't I just stay up a few more minutes? I don't want to go to bed.

Susan made me mad. She always says mean things.

I have too much homework. I hate homework.

Why do we have to eat this? I hate this.

I want to go play with my friends. Why can't I go play with them?

I hate cleaning my room. It's my room. Why can't I keep it the way I want?

My tooth hurts. Can you see if something is wrong with it?

I hurt my toe. Will you pray it stops hurting?

Thank you for fixing dinner for us. You're a good cook.

Can I help you clean off the table?

What time do I need to wake up for church?

Can we have a family night and watch a movie together?

I really like our family. I'm glad I'm part of this family.

I appreciate you.

I'm so thankful for God's love.

I'm glad God gave us this home.

God is so good.

Why do we have to eat mushrooms. They are so icky.

I don't want to brush my teeth every morning. It's annoying.

Please don't make me read that long book. I don't want to.

Attend

For Mom and Dad
Preparing Our Hearts

Scripture: Hebrews 10:24-25; 1 Corinthians 12

I've attended church my whole life since I was an infant. I became a Christian when I was seven years old and was called to ministry not long after that. My parents laughed when I told them I needed to take piano lessons because I was going to marry a pastor. (I never did get to take piano lessons until seminary, and by then, it was a little late to master the instrument.) Even with all of that, I did not feel a part of the church body until our church formed a youth council. We met and helped plan fundraisers and activities for the youth. Our youth group came to life like never before. What is even more amazing to me is that most of our youth group either wound up becoming pastors, missionaries, or going on short-term international mission trips as adults. All of the group that I've kept in touch with have remained faithful churchgoers, often taking on leadership in their churches. Helping our children and others feel a part of the Body of Christ within our churches is so important to the health of the church and to our individual health as followers of Christ. Belonging to a body of believers makes us part of a family where we can grow in our faith and encourage each other. As we work together in ministry through the church, we can become more Christlike and help each other do the same.

God is very clear that he wants us in fellowship with other Christians. We cannot obey many of the commands given to us as believers unless we are meeting together. God tells us that iron sharpens iron (Proverbs 27:17). When we meet together, we help one another grow and become more Christlike. We are told to love one another, encourage one another, spur one another on to good works (John 13:34, 1 Thessalonians 5:11, Hebrews 10:24). We cannot do these when we don't meet.

In addition, we all are an important part of the body of Christ which is seen in action within the local body of believers. Our churches need us and miss us when we aren't there, and the same goes for our children.

Going to church is also tremendously important in a child's life. Proverbs 22:6 says for us to help a child know how they should live.

There are a few articles that you may want to read and two of my podcasts you may want to listen to that deal with this topic. If you go to my website: terriehellardbrown.com and look under podcasts, check out my interviews with Megan Hill. She has written extensively about children and going to church.

Prayer: Pray that God will lead you to a healthy, Bible-believing congregation that loves children. Pray that God will give you a strong desire to be involved in your local church.

Preparing to Parent

Since COVID, some parents have found it difficult to return to attending church. Some are still very concerned about the spread of COVID or other viruses, they feel the world, including church, just doesn't seem safe for our kids anymore.

We are torn between our desire to obey God and be in fellowship with other Christians and making sure our children are safe. Wherever our children go, we can make sure that normal safety and cleanliness is part of the standard practice of the church, school, or daycare. However, obsessing over it all does not really glorify God. I hear God saying to us, "Where is your faith." We don't want to be careless and reckless, but we want to trust God at the same time. Most places today are very careful and conscious of safety and cleanliness protocols, especially churches.

For the Family
Enjoying the Lesson Together

Scripture: Hebrews 10:24-25; 1 Corinthians 12
(remember to choose a verse as your family memory verse with each lesson)

Object Lesson: The Church Is a Body

You can decide how you want to accomplish this object lesson. You can put a sticker or tie a string on one child's arm, another's leg, your hand, or blindfold one person. Wherever the sticker or string is, that part of a person's body is off-limits, and they cannot use it.

Set up a simple obstacle course in the living room or in the yard. Have each child try to get through it without using the off-limits part of their body.

Ask: Was it difficult to complete the obstacle course? Why? What would have made it easier or more fun?

Let's try it again. This time I want all of us to work together. The one with the use of both hands can help move things out of the way for the other person. The ones who aren't blindfolded can help the blindfolded person walk through without falling. Use the abilities you have to help each other succeed through the course.

The Bible talks about the church as the body of Christ. Each part of the body has a purpose, and together everyone in church helps accomplish the ministries and work God is wanting to do in our lives and in our community.

Share your jobs you've done at church. Talk about ways children can help or bless others in church: answering questions the Sunday School teacher asks, listening attentively, greeting guests, encouraging someone with kind words, holding the door open for someone, helping set the tables at the potluck, helping someone carry something, smiling — there are many simple ways children can make a big difference in church.

Prayer/Song/Poem: Church Fingerplay

    Do you know the fingerplay for the church?
    Hands together with fingers interlocked inside: Here's the church
    First fingers up: Here's the steeple
    Open the door: open the thumbs
    And here's all the people: all the fingers are the people

Activity: Church Tour

If you are attending a new church, see if you can make an appointment with the pastor to visit the church and to show the children their classrooms and where everything is.

Even if you've been members for a while, you may still want to visit the pastor or a staff member and let your children see parts of the church they may not have seen before and talk about who does what in the church.

We can also do a virtual tour by visiting the church's website, looking at the different staff members and what they do.

Read *Meg Is Not Alone* together.

Picture Books: *Little Mole Goes to School* by Glenys Nellist, *Meg Is Not Alone* by Megan Hill, *When I Go to Church, I Belong* by Elrena Evans, *God Made Me for Worship* by Jared Kennedy

Bring

For Mom and Dad
Preparing our Hearts

Scripture: 2 Corinthians 9:7; 1 Chronicles 29:15-17; Matthew 6:21; 1 Timothy 6:10

Our pastor started his sermon with an example of a person going to the doctor. They have a pain in their side. The doctor says, "It's not supposed to hurt there." He runs tests to find out what's wrong and how to heal the person. He made the analogy to people when they hear a sermon about money. People groan and hate hearing about giving. He says, "It's not supposed to hurt there." Our pastor warned if hearing about giving to God hurts us, something isn't right with our walk with God, and we need to find what the problem is. He reminded us that all we have belongs to the Lord anyway, and he asked us to examine why we are bothered by the topic of giving to the Lord.

He's right. The Bible warns us about loving money and tells us where our treasure is, that's where our hearts will be. God loves for us to give with hearts of joy, love, and absolute happiness. He always blesses us when we give. Some take that to mean we give money so God will give us more money. That is not what the scriptures say or mean. It is a popular misuse of scripture by some, but the truth is, we cannot outgive God. He always blesses us abundantly more when we give. God's blessing is not always in monetary returns, but it is often in so many other ways.

Our attitude in giving should be like the Israelites in 1 Chronicles. What a beautiful picture of joyful giving. When we read these passages, we must ask ourselves where our own heart is, how we feel about giving, and why we give. Our attitudes about giving reflect so much of where we are in our walk with God. It is like the thermometer showing we have a problem in our spiritual health, or, like my pastor said, "It's not supposed to hurt there."

Prayer: If it hurts to give, we should ask God to show us why. Is it a matter of distrust or lack of faith? Is it because we are selfish or uncommitted? Do we resent the expectation and see giving as an obligation? IF so, this might be a problem in our love for God possibly. Once we know why we feel the way we do, we can pray specifically about it and seek God's help and heart in our giving.

Preparing to Parent

Giving is an interesting topic to approach with children. It seems that some children enjoy giving so much that they will give away their toys, food, or anything just to bless others, and some have a hard time giving away anything without feeling a bit put out. Their attitudes are ultimately something God will have to deal with, but we can help them learn the power of giving, sowing and reaping, and being cheerful about it—at least we can try.

The best way, of course, is for us to set the example. The second way is to help them understand that they can have faith in our provision and in God's. The third way we can help them is to give them opportunities to give starting with handing them the offering to put into the plate on Sundays and allowing them to be a part of going through their toys and clothes a couple times a year to give some away to charities or thrift shops. We create a culture of giving in our families when we do these things.

For the Family
Enjoying the Lesson Together

Scripture: Psalm 96:8; 2 Corinthians 9:7; Mark 12:41-44
(remember to choose a verse as your family memory verse with each lesson)

Object Lesson: Skittles and Blocks

For this object lesson, prepare a little box or bag for each child giving them skittles (or other colorful candy such as M&Ms or jellybeans) and small blocks per child. For some, give them a lot of each item, and for others, only give them two. You can mix it up and give one child a bunch of blocks but only two candies, and another two blocks and several candies.

You will need a white plate and water

Tell the story of the widow giving the two small coins. Ask what happens when we each give all we have to God? Our faith grows, and we spread God's love to the world. When we give, even if it is just a little, it can make a big difference.

Have each child give their candies by putting them on the plate. They can choose how many they give. Talk about how if you have ten candies and give three you are generous, but if you only have two and give both, you are more generous. Of course, if they have ten and give ten, they are just like the widow who gave all she had.

Put the candies around the edge of the plate.

Pour water in the bottom of the plate to where it touches the bottom of each candy but doesn't cover them.

Within just a few minutes, the food coloring will begin to spread through the water.

Talk about how when we each give, we make a difference together. Even if we only have a small amount to give, it can make a big difference.

Of course, giving your candies for the experiment did not take a lot of faith, but when we give all we have, God is honored because we show how much we trust him to provide for our needs. The widow gave all she had because she knew God would meet her needs. Her faith was so strong.

Have each child pull out their blocks. Can you build a building with your blocks? Not really. Even if a child has several blocks, how could they make a bigger, nicer building? What can we do?

By now, they should understand that if they give their blocks and others give theirs, together they can build a nice building. Those who have more may need to give more.

Let the whole family work together to build a building and celebrate their creation.

Ask each child how they felt when they gave their candies and blocks. Was it hard to give? Why was it easy if it was easy? Why was it hard if it was hard? Do you like to give to God? What can we give to God? What does God do with what we give to him?

You may want to reference the little boy and his lunch and how giving his lunch enabled God to multiply his gift to feed more than 5000 people with leftovers (Matthew 14). And the story of the widow and the oil when she shared with Elisha (2 Kings 4).

Prayer/Song/Poem: Pray that we can all be cheerful givers, and that God would multiply and use what we give to build his kingdom.

Activity: Banks

Supplies needed:
One tall and two short pringle cans per child (or one tall can per child if you want a simple bank)
Colored paper
Stickers

Scissors
Crayons or markers
Tape or glue
Large rubber bands

Cut slits in each lid.

Each child will decorate their own cans, and if doing three cans, the tallest is for their regular money for spending and saving, but one shorter can will be for saving a tithe or offering. The other shorter can (optional) will be for saving for a special purpose (missions, Christmas, college, a trip). Write or use sticker letters to label each can.

You can put a large rubber band around the cans to keep them together.

Start saving!

Reiterate that our word for this lesson is "bring." Each week we should prepare ahead of time what we will bring to give in the offering at church. Bringing means we prepare.

Picture Books: *Stone Soup* by Marcia Brown, *My Money Bunnies* by Mike Michalowicz, *Give* by Jen Arena

Worship (Only God)

For Mom and Dad
Preparing Our Hearts

Scripture: Romans 12:1-2, John 4:23-24

One of my imperatives for myself is to worship authentically. I have led worship and shared special music and done concerts in my ministry. I've taught and spoken on many types of platforms, and I try very hard to take that seriously. One time when I was in college, I was serving on a revival team which meant that a team of us would go out for the weekend to a little country church and share for several special services. I was the soloist. One week I forgot we had an event that weekend. I had a terrible week and was really far from God. I was not focused at all. It was the worst weekend. I felt guilty and out of sorts. I felt ill-prepared and embarrassed that I was not giving these people what they deserved. I swore I would never do that again. Worship is something we owe God, and I don't ever want it to be a "going through the motions" activity.

We sometimes think of singing and listening to a preacher as worship, but we should recognize that worship is much more. For one thing, a song means nothing without the heart behind it. Listening to a preacher does nothing if we don't allow the Holy Spirit to work through the words that are shared and then apply them to our lives. Worship is a matter of our minds, hearts, and actions. According to Romans 12:1-2 it is a matter of our minds and bodies. Worship is commitment, exclusively and single-mindedly set aside to a purpose or service to God and submission to his ways, not our own ways.

The songs, the words, the prayers, and any expression of worship must first begin with our true commitment to God so that the songs are an outpouring and expression of what is already happening in our hearts and minds. Worship involves our spirits and God's truth (John 4:23-24).

Today, with so many claiming that their desires outweigh God's plans, Romans 12 really speaks to us. In addition, when our bodies are committed to God, that means He can send us where He wants us, and we can serve with our hearts, souls, minds, and strength. Our lives will reflect worship, and our actions become worship to the God we love and serve.

Prayer: We can ask God to renew our minds to help us understand His perfect will and direction for our lives. We can pray for the faith we need to be able to step out where God leads.

Preparing to Parent

Since these "Preparing to Parent" sections are meant to give parents, things to reflect on when approaching the topic for the lesson, we should consider a few items regarding worship.

First, as John 4:23-24 says, those who worship God worship Him in spirit and truth. Along those lines, we should evaluate the level of our children's spiritual development to know how much to teach them about worship. Are they ready to participate in worship, or do we simply model the actions which they copy without understanding?

Second, truth must be at the core of our worship and theirs. We need to take time to evaluate what we do in worship and what we believe. Are there some activities or teachings that really aren't part of Scripture? Do we worship the way we do out of habit, religious fear, or church tradition? Do we see this kind of worship in Scripture? Are we worshiping a true image of God? Or have we in some ways made God into an image of our own design? We should periodically evaluate our worship in this way because it is easy to grab onto ideas that sound good but are not true to the Bible. Churches, if they don't already, should adopt a habit of evaluating if they are staying true to the God of Scripture and their worship reflects commitment to the One True God.

As we guide our children into worship and following Christ, we can rest in the knowledge that we are teaching them to worship biblically when we self-evaluate, and they can see in Scripture the truth of what we are teaching. As they become older, this becomes vital. So many are walking away from faith for many reasons, but one reason we see again and again is because of wrong teaching. Young adults feel they've been lied to. Some don't know who to trust, and they are so confused they don't want to trust any church.

Worshiping in truth also means that we are not putting on a show of worship, but we are truly worshiping. That is why evaluating where our children are in their walk is important. If they are only mimicking what they see, and it is not truly coming from their hearts, they need to be able to understand the difference between looking like we're worshiping and actually worshiping.

Third, we need to help our children understand the difference between respect, honor, and worship. We honor our parents and grandparents and respect all people, but we only worship God. So, what is the difference between the three? The first object lesson focuses on these definitions.

Fourth, we may need to help our children understand the difference between worshiping the Creator and worshiping His creation.

The key to all these considerations is simply knowing our children, allowing them to express their faith in their own words so we grasp where they are in understanding, and allowing the Holy Spirit to give us His wisdom as parents. We can do this with His help.

For the Family
Enjoying the Lesson Together

Scripture: Exodus 20:12; 1Peter 2:17; Col. 3:4; Hebrews 12:28
  (remember to choose a verse as your family memory verse with each lesson)

Object Lesson: Honor, Respect, or Worship

> Supplies needed:
> A picture of a grandmother or grandfather
> Bible
> Candy
> Whatever other objects your child values or cherishes

1. Place these items in the order of what is most important to you.
2. In the bible, Matthew tells us that where our treasure is, our heart will be there also. A treasure is something more important than regular things. In other words, the thing I value most will be what my heart will focus on and will be the thing that becomes most important in my life.
3. Who should be most important in our lives?
4. Sometimes we may not keep God first. What should we do when we realize we've got things out of order?
5. Do we need to be afraid that God is going to be angry or not love us anymore if we put something ahead of him? That's kind of a tricky question because God ALWAYS loves us. He never stops loving us. But when his people in the Bible worshiped idols, and did not repent, God did punish them. The key is that they did not repent when God confronted them for worshipping the wrong things. When we realize we've had things in the wrong order, we need to ask God to forgive us and put him in first place again.
6. Does that mean we can't say we love ice cream or that we think our grandma is wonderful? No, we can love lots of things and appreciate lots of people, but God is number one in our lives. We love, adore, and give ourselves to serve him alone.
7. In fact, we thank God for ice cream and a wonderful grandma. They are blessings from him.
8. How do we worship God? 1 Samuel 15:22; 1 Chronicles 16:23-31; Hebrews 12:28; Psalm 100 (Make a list of ways we can express worship, explaining any that need clarification and then spend time as a family worshiping together. If you are uncomfortable with this or not quite sure how to do it, choose several items such as praise, thanksgiving, and exalting and sing a song together praising God, then pray thanking God, and end with a song that exalts his name.) Now, acknowledge that he is God. Recognize who he is and

what his character is. This can revolve around the names of God that reveal who he is. We can worship him as our healer, provider, shelter, comforter, wisdom, and life. He wants us to know He has covered us, so we know he is our savior, salvation, the resurrection, and the life. He has provided the way through what Jesus did for us. We can rest and know that He loves us fully — completely forever. He is the alpha and the omega, the beginning and the end which reminds us that God is eternal, and he will never leave us nor forsake us. He is always with us even throughout eternity. Do you feel how wonderful that is?

Prayer/Song/Poem: A song you may want to learn together is "Thanks and Praise" by Songs from the Soil. Sovereign Grace has a great song called "Sing" that is fun, well, to sing.

Activity: Painted Rocks

In Luke 19:40 Jesus tells those listening that if people refused to praise God, the rocks would cry out praises. Even though this is not considered literal in that rocks would being singing God's praises, it is a reminder that we should praise God.

For our activity today, we will paint rocks to remind us to praise God every day.

Supplies needed:
    Flat, smooth rocks
    Paint pens or paint and brushes
    Mod Podge or some sort of sealant for parents to add once the paint is dry (Clear Elmer's Glue works too)

Let each child paint a rock with something that will remind them to praise God. They may want to write "praise" or "worship" or a reference such as "Psalm 100" on them.

Picture Books: *Psalms of Praise* by Danielle Hitchen, *The Quest for True Worship* by Paul Atem, *My Little One, Let's Talk about Worship* by Kacy Bristol,

Worship (the Creator)

For Mom and Dad
Preparing Our Hearts

Scripture: Romans 1:23, 25; John 4:23-24

I tend to be a workaholic. I love what I do, and much of what I do is ministry related. So, it is easy to justify it in my mind. (Truthfully, we can justify and rationalize almost anything — we're good at that). So, I must have accountability with others, and I often offer up my whole career to God. I tell him I will walk away from it all if he tells me to. And I mean it. Because I do not want to be a stumbling block to others or to myself. My husband, board of directors, and business builder team hold me accountable. I'm not perfect at it, but I'm better. I trust God to show me when I've put what I'm doing ahead of following him. When God reveals something to us that we are putting on the throne of our lives — God's rightful place — we immediately must repent and obey God because putting anything in God's place is idolatry.

It may not be something we think of often in the US, but in other places we become keenly aware of the idols people worship. In Taiwan, they mostly worshipped idols resembling what we might imagine demons look like, and even the Taiwanese often acknowledge that they are worshiping or at least trying to appease demons.

However, in our culture, idols might sneak up on us unnoticed like becoming a workaholic. Sometimes we even put a Christian spin on them such as some of the New Thought practices of affirmations, "manifesting" wealth and health, and trying to live our "best life" supposedly all in the name of Jesus ignoring that it is contrary to what Jesus taught. If we pay attention, and we let the Holy Spirit show us, we can begin to see where idols may be lurking in our own lives.

The most common idol I've seen among Christians is the idol of self. We exercise and eat right to try to stay healthy, which is important and good. But some go too far. The pursuit of some sort of imagined perfection becomes a god and an obsession taking up our time, money, and focus to the point that it consumes people. Or, in trying to be a loving Christian, we compromise the teachings of the Bible and affirm sinfulness as good. It's a "live your truth," "you're perfect just as you are," "you do you" mentality that some Christians have adopted. Focusing on self-esteem and rights tend to be at the center of much of this theology.

Of course, we probably all know those who are caught in the trap of money, workaholism, or other isms of addiction. Whenever we are controlled by something, it has become a sort of a god in our life.

How can we guard our hearts, renew our minds, and keep our hearts focused on our First Love? How can we keep fear and the pursuit of spiritual formulas for success from taking over the sovereign work of God in our lives?

We must rely on prayer and repentance. When the Holy Spirit shows us that we've let something take over his rightful place, we repent. When we recognize we are thinking wrong, we ask God to help us to renew our minds so that we can think correctly.

It happens to the best of us if we aren't careful. Thinking about whether we are making something an idol isn't something that should consume us or worry us. However, it is something we should check on periodically in prayer.

Just like getting a checkup at the doctor or dentist's offices, we should get a check up on our spiritual condition. The best way is to read our Bibles, and we can easily hear the Holy Spirit telling us when we're getting off track. We must trust God. He wants us to stay close to him and worship only him. He will help us.

Prayer: We should ask God to reveal anywhere in our lives that we are putting something in his place in our lives. We can ask him to show us what we're basing our decisions on—are we making decisions based on God's word, on fear, what others think, or our own reasoning? Then, if we have need, let's repent and get back in step with following him faithfully. And if we're not out of step, rejoice! Praise God for his goodness and faithfulness.

Preparing to Parent

With little children, this may not be an issue yet. However, as our children get older, we begin to see the treasures that threaten to steal their hearts, especially when crushes and dating come into the picture.

We must begin praying now. And we need to teach our children from a young age the lessons we're doing now. Today's lesson will help them think about creation vs Creator. Which are we worshipping? This lesson can transfer into the life of a pre-teen or teen as they begin to wrestle with priorities and faith.

For the Family
Enjoying the Lesson Together

Scripture: Romans 1:20, Psalms 19:1-6

Object Lesson: Nature Trip

For this lesson, going to the mountains, lake, or other area in nature to worship will help families experience worship for our Creator. Ideally, if this can be a camping trip for the weekend or overnight, the family can do several activities to drive home the lesson of worshiping our Creator.

First object lesson/activity is to look at nature and see that God is an amazing Creator.

Second object lesson/activity is to create some art: paint a picture or draw one which then reminds us for every "work of art" there is an artist — the art didn't create itself. Nature shows us that there is a Creator.

Third object lesson/activity: fingerprints. If you can use a fingerprint kit, that's even cooler, but we can make fingerprint art where our artwork literally shows the fingerprints of the artist. When we see nature, we see God's fingerprints on our world.

We used to always go to the mountains for retreats. It was a time of focusing on worship and a time of renewal. Something about being in the mountains was refreshing physically and spiritually.

Throughout scripture we see different men of God going to worship in the mountains. Then, we also see those who worshipped idols setting up their items of worship in the "high places." It seems like it is meant to be a slap in God's face as people worship idols where other people have always worshipped God. Even Jesus would get away to the mountains to pray (Matthew 14:23, Luke 6:12; Luke 9:28)

Another temptation is to look at nature, seeing how beautiful it is, and begin to worship it rather than the God who created it. We certainly can admire the beauty of God's creation, but as we see it, our hearts and minds will usually start thanking God for the beauty we see. Most of the time in today's cultures, we see the shift to worshiping nature more in an obsession about conservation or by caring more about an animal over concern for people.

As we come to the mountains or other nature area, we want to get away from our normal lives and focus on worshiping God. We want to see each sunrise, flower, butterfly, tree, and deer as a fingerprint. They remind us that we have a wonderful Creator who makes beautiful things including us. We can think of the sunrise as whispering to us, "Good morning, worship God and thank him for a new day." We can imagine that the butterfly flits around singing, "Worship the Lord with all your heart. He is our wonderful Creator." We can hear those rocks crying out praise to God like Jesus says in Luke 19:40, "Praise God. Give him the glory he deserves."

In addition, just as the rest of nature brings glory to God and points to his goodness, we should too. What are ways we can bring glory to God? How can we show God's goodness to others?

Prayer/Song/Poem: One of the main ways people worshiped God on the mountains was to pray. We can spend some time in prayer together praising God and asking him to draw us closer to him.

Activity: Painting or Drawing

Create art and create fingerprint art. Write one of these verses on the artwork: Romans 1:20, Psalms 19:1-6

Picture Books: *Psalms of Praise* by Danielle Hitchen, *The Quest for True Worship* by Paul Atem, *My Little One, Let's Talk about Worship* by Kacy Bristol

Worship

For Mom and Dad
Preparing Our Hearts

Scripture: Genesis 22:1-18; Romans 12:1-2; Ephesians 2:10

We've always joked that the problem with living sacrifices is they keep climbing off the altar. However, that's kind of true. It was as close to an Abraham and Isaac situation that we've come to in our lives. We were applying to pastor a church in Jakarta, Indonesia. We felt strongly that we were supposed to apply, but in the process, we learned more about the country and culture, and the Mama Bear in me became very concerned for our cubs. Going to a predominately Muslim country that was beginning to experience some political unrest freaked me out. I prayed, and I climbed back and forth on and off the altar for a while until I felt the matter settled in my heart. We began to prepare to move overseas by selling most of our electrical items since the electricity was different there, getting renewed passports, and looking into what immunizations we needed to get. The night everything was to be finalized, the door slammed shut. The deciding committee had changed their decision to a 50/50 split since the political situation there was becoming more serious. They had become concerned about bringing a family with young children into the unrest and the constant evacuations. We were shocked, but we prayed. We knew in our hearts God had a plan. Within two days, we were looking at Taiwan as that door flew open wide.

According to scripture, obedience and surrender are acts of worship. Even though God didn't take us there, as we prepared for the possible move to Jakarta, we felt a sense of worship in our decision to honor God with our family's lives.

Obedience is better than sacrifice. Surrender speaks to the condition of our hearts before God rather than just offering a thing on the altar. God wants us to offer ourselves so that he can use our lives for his glory and purposes. Romans 12 makes it clear that surrender is real worship.

As we examine our hearts and seek to live a life that honors and glorifies God, we know that we must choose to surrender our wills, our desires, and our plans to God. Often that means we must choose to surrender daily, and sometimes when surrender requires sacrifice and battling our selfish desires, we may need to surrender moment by moment. Surrender can be painful. It is not always easy—in fact, it is seldom easy to surrender our wills. We don't often talk about how painful obedience can be. Our wills are strong, and denying them is not only difficult, but it hurts. It is a battle.

When we look at Abraham, we can recognize how hard and painful obedience and surrender can be. Abraham finally saw his promised child born. Isaac was Sarah's and his joy and proof that God always keeps his promises. Then, God told him to sacrifice Isaac. Abraham knew Isaac was the promised child, and he knew that God keeps his promises. So, he obeyed. He probably wasn't sure what to think. He probably didn't understand what God was doing at all. He just knew the right response was obedience, surrender, and a very real sacrifice.

We also see a willing Isaac. It doesn't seem that Abraham had to tackle his son to put him on the altar. It seems clear that Isaac had the same kind of faith that his father modeled for him.

Both men seem to understand that God can be trusted, and they needed to obey him even when it made no sense to them.

We can almost hear the collective sigh of relief when the angel stops Abraham's hand, and they see the ram in the thicket. We can only imagine the worship that took place as they sacrificed that ram. In the whole encounter, both Abraham and Isaac learned that God truly does keep his promises, he is uncompromising in requiring obedience, and God provides when we are.

We may find it difficult to put ourselves in their places especially since we aren't used to offering sacrifices as part of our worship. However, we can understand how hard it is to put our children in God's hands and let them make their choices and mistakes. We know how easy it is to become consumed with parenting that everything else seems to fall by the wayside. However, we also know how much we rely on God as we parent. We pray continually seeking wisdom and help in making the right decisions for our children. Sometimes parenting and discipleship can feel like a tug of war for our attention and for our hearts. The reality is, discipleship is also part of parenting. Christ needs to be Lord of our parenting, Lord of our marriages, and Lord of our daily decisions and actions. This is how our daily activities become worship like Romans 12 says.

That's the key to all of this. Worship is honoring God with our whole lives: our hearts, minds, souls, and strength. It is surrendering our wills to follow God's will. It is living a life that glorifies God, which means to make his name known. May we understand that we were created for worship in every moment of our lives.

Prayer: We should pray that we can be true living sacrifices staying on the alter in obedience to Christ. We pray that our lives honor and glorify God each day.

Preparing to Parent

Parenting our children to help them learn surrender and obedience to Christ is, quite frankly, not something we can teach them well. They must learn from our example and Scripture, but mostly they must learn from the guidance of the Holy Spirit to deny themselves and follow him. We can teach them the verses. We can show them how we live out our faith. We can show them how we choose God's ways rather than our own selfish desires. But we cannot pretend to be the Holy Spirit and somehow make them obey. If we force compliance, we must understand that is not true obedience. Obedience is a matter of the heart as much as it is a matter of right actions.

As far as helping them grasp the lessons of denying self, we can raise them to understand delayed gratification which will help them as they grow in their faith later. Waiting is a character-building activity that has great benefits. Isaac had to 'wait' because he asked where the sacrifice was and Abraham only told him God will provide one. And even while he 'waited' for God's provision, he remained obedient and climbed onto the alter. So, we can consider ways to help our children learn to wait gracefully, and, in that, learn to deny themselves.

For the Family

Enjoying the Lesson Together

Scripture: Isaiah 1: 18; Romans 12:1-2; Matthew 4:16

(remember to choose a verse as your family memory verse with each lesson)

Object Lesson: Obedient Lives Worship God and Shine His Light

Supplies needed:
Two clear glasses
Vegetable oil
Water
Red food coloring
A chopstick, long spoon, or something to stir with
Two cell phones (Don't worry. They should not get wet.)

Fill one cup with water and the other fill only about 1/3 to ½ with water.

You can put the glasses on the cell phones with the flashlights on shining into the cups or you can wait to do it after reading Matthew 4:16.

When each of us is born, we are born as sinful people who choose to disobey God's rules.
Add red food coloring representing sin to both glasses of water.

We are separated from God, and only when we choose to accept God's forgiveness and follow Jesus does God fill our lives with his Spirit and his love.

Pour oil into the second cup only as you say this. Try to pour the oil with as few air bubbles as possible. Gently stir the oil and water together. Both water and oil should look red with "sin."

Read Isaiah 1:18.

The oil represents the change God brings in our lives. We are still living in the world, but we have been changed by God.

At first, they are mixed together but then the oil separates. At first the redness of the sin is in the oil, but it is removed and is only in the water. When God forgives us, he forgives us completely removing the sin from our lives.

Read Romans 12:1-2.

As God becomes the Lord of our lives, we are separated from the world like the oil separates from the water. The Bible calls this separation holiness, which means we are set apart. We are still living in the world, but we are separate from it.

When we follow Christ, our lives shine God's love to the world, and what we do is considered worship to God—we honor him with our whole lives.

Read Matthew 4:16

Turn on the flashlights on each phone and place the cups over the flashlights if you haven't done that already. It should shine up through the liquid in the cups. The light should glow through the oil. You should only see a little light in the water, with barely any shining. It definitely does not glow like it does in the oil.

So, with what you've seen in this lesson, how do we worship God with our whole lives? How do we live as living sacrifices?

Prayer/Song/Poem: "Shine a Light" from Kids on the Move

Activity: Reflection and Shining Light

>Supplies Needed:
>Flashlights
>Mirrors
>Other reflective surfaces such as a cookie sheet, glass of water, prism, different colors of paper

Jesus said we are the light of the world. But we don't shine our own light. We reflect God's light when we obey him.

Let the children have fun for a while just shining the light on different objects, and then have them shine their flashlight on a bright piece of paper (neon colored, if possible, white or bright yellow otherwise). Write the words "Living Sacrifice" on the paper. Shine the light on it, and you'll see how the light and even the color is reflected off the paper.

Have a dark piece of paper with "Disobedient" written on it and see how the light does not reflect off the paper. The light makes the paper brighter. God's light always reveals our sin and reminds us to ask for forgiveness. But when we obey God and are living sacrifices, our lives can reflect God's love to others. Shine the light on the bright paper again.

End with a short prayer and allow the children to continue playing with the flashlights if they want.

Picture Books: *Psalms of Praise* by Danielle Hitchen, *The Quest for True Worship* by Paul Atem, *My Little One, Let's Talk about Worship* by Kacy Bristol

Praise

For Mom and Dad
Preparing our Hearts

Scripture: Psalm 146:1-2, Psalm 150:1-6, 1 Peter1:3, James 3:9-10

My friend and I were walking down the alley behind our church in Taipei when this lovely woman walked by and smiled at us. She said, "You are very fat" to both of us. In my mind, I was thinking of all kinds of unkind responses to her observation when she asked, "Do you go to this church?" Ugh! I changed my thoughts immediately. We answered yes to her question, and we joked later saying through gritted teeth, "God loves you."

It can seem easy for us to be upset with others but still give praise to God in our prayers and worship. However, the Bible says that's not right. Admittedly, it is hard sometimes. We get angry or hurt, and we want to lash out at the person causing the pain, get revenge, or at least hit them with a good zinger that stings. But God calls us to do better. If we see people as he sees them, and if we love them like he does, we may still get upset and hurt, but our response would be to take that to him in prayer. Our words and actions toward others would be more gracious. If we are really hurt and can't let go of it, we can talk to the person and work to reconcile with them, but when we do, we don't react with emotion and curses, but rather with an attitude of working together to resolve your misunderstanding.

John Piper says every time he talks to a person or prepares a sermon, his goal is "... to awaken affections for God and satisfy them with God." That is powerful. If our goal in whatever interaction we have with people becomes a goal like that, we would find that we praise God even in the difficult interactions as we point them to Christ. What a different life many of us would live if we had this kind of attitude and let go of the self-focused concerns that often bombard our minds.

We would find such joy and freedom in praising God when we've glorified him among the people we encounter each day. God says the Holy Spirit will guide and help us, and we surely need to rely on him. We can ask him to help in all circumstances and relationships.

Prayer: We can pray for God's help so that we are filled with love for people. We can pray for hearts filled with praise for God and a desire to make his name known among the people. God can help our focus and attitude change.

Preparing to Parent

As we prepare to parent, we must examine our own hearts. Beyond just the lesson today, we need to make sure our example is solid—that we aren't saying and teaching one thing but presenting a different example for our children to see. They will follow our actions more than our words.

If we are guilty of cursing people and situations and still trying to help our children learn to praise God, they will see the hypocrisy in our worship. We must get our hearts right. We must share a true example of worship and praise.

God is good. He will help us, and we can admit when we fail. We can tell our children that we shouldn't have said what we said. They need to see a genuine heart more than a perfect performance. We can do this, with God's help and truth.

For the Family
Enjoying the Lesson Together

Scripture: Psalm 146:1-2, Psalm 150:1-6, 1 Peter1:3
   (remember to choose a verse as your family memory verse with each lesson)

Object Lesson: Letters of Praise

Write each of your family members a letter of praise. Read it out loud during your time together. Ask each person how they felt when you praised them. Ask how they think God feels when we praise him.

You wrote a letter, but how can we praise each other in different ways? How can we praise God in different ways? What is one of the main ways the Bible mentions for praising God? Read the verses from Psalm 146.

Prayer/Song/Poem: Sing a song or praise to God. If your family can write one of your own, that would be amazing, but if not, here are a few to choose from:

"Psalm 150 (Praise the Lord)" by Keith and Kristen Getty

"Sing" by Sovereign Grace Music

Kids songs —

"Praise Him, Praise Him, All Ye Little Children"

"Praise Him"—"Praise Him in the Morning, Praise Him in the Noontime, Praise Him When the Sun Goes Down"

"We Will Sing Praise (To the Lord Our Creator)"

Activity: Praise band

For a fun activity, have a praise and worship time as a family, and have fun with it. We can bring out instruments, pots and pans, banners, or whatever would be wonderful to use in praising God. Our kids will love dancing and singing, playing instruments, and waving banners.

If you don't have banners to wave, maybe your family can create some for times like these. Then each child can hang them on their bedroom wall.

Banners can be made several ways, but each should have words of praise on them. We aren't making dance flags, but rather banners that declare a word of praise to God, a name of God, or a characteristic of God.

The most elaborate banner we've made used parachute fabric in bright colors where we cut out letters and designs and sewed them onto the background fabric.

We can make simpler ones by ironing on letters and cut-out designs

A simpler version is to cut a pillowcase in two (preferably a non-wrinkle kind) and surge or sew the edges. Then, let the children use crayons to draw and write on their piece of fabric. After they finish, lay their crayon design face down on wax paper or parchment paper, and put a towel or paper over the back of it and iron the design to melt it into the fabric and make it permanent.

The simplest banner is to get nice, white paper napkins (they come in a box in most grocery stores). Have children fold them in different ways, and then dip parts of it into food coloring and vinegar mixture (like for dying eggs). Carefully unfold each one and let it dry. Once dry, children can use pens to write words of praise on them. We used chopsticks to hang them by just gluing the paper napkin to the chopstick and tying the ends of a piece of yarn to each end of the chopstick to make a hanger.

Picture Books: *Psalms of Praise* by Danielle Hitchens, *God Made Me for Worship* by Jared Kennedy, *Let's Make a Joyful Noise to the Lord* by Karma Wilson

Abide

For Mom & Dad
Preparing Our Hearts

Scripture: John 15

Our first two children were born with clefts, and we were thrown into a whirlwind of doctors' appointments, social workers, and occupational therapy almost from day one. It was more than we could handle, and it was much more than we expected. In fact, when our first daughter was born, I looked at her cleft and naively thought we'd simply go to the doctor and have him sew her lip shut and be done. I never expected the years of surgeries, speech therapy, and occupational therapy. Once I felt I had a handle on all of that, then we found out both have autism, and later their youngest brother also was diagnosed with autism. It slowed down the surgical process and opened up a whole new realm of issues and situations to deal with.

Usually when we think of abiding in Christ, we think of spiritual things. We think of ministry and sharing our faith, but I understood the verse that says, "Apart from me, you can do nothing" more than I ever did in ministry with just walking through the work of being a parent. I could not have done it without Christ. One person said I had a pioneer spirit because I was so strong and calm through it all. I almost laughed because I knew, it was all God.

John 15 contains Jesus' last teaching before the Passion Week. He teaches the most vital lesson on discipleship as he tells his Disciples and us that we must abide/remain in him. Jesus tells us that our strength and power to do the work he's called us to can only be found by remaining in him. Apart from him, we can do nothing. So, the question becomes, as Hudson

Taylor, renowned missionary to China spent his life trying to grasp and understand, how do we abide? What does that mean? What does that look like in a Christian's daily walk?

To abide in the love of Christ, as verse 9 tells us, means we accept his love for us and remain in it, yielding our behavior to it. His love becomes our resting place, the place where we live our lives and the place from which, hopefully, we parent our children. All that we do comes from us living our lives in God's presence and with the Holy Spirit's guidance, strength, and help.

Abiding or remaining in God and in his love will bring us peace, strength, inspiration, wisdom, and insight.

Prayer: Ask God to show you ways you can continually abide/remain in his presence throughout the day. Take time to feel his peace and strength with you even now as you pray.

Preparing to Parent

With all that is being taught about God even through picture books, we should check that our children are understanding. One of the concepts that can be misunderstood and that is being taught incorrectly are the ideas of God's omnipresence, pantheism, and panentheism. God is everywhere, and Psalm 139 teaches our children that God is everywhere, and God is always with them. However, some would teach that God is in everything or that everything has a spirit in it, even trees and inanimate objects as well as animals. Or they teach that nature is part of God even though they are separate. In historical Christianity, God is the Creator of nature but is not part of nature. He is separate and greater than all of creation. We may see God's fingerprints in His creation — because we have creation, we know there is a Creator. However, God is not in the tree. And the tree is not part of God. And we cannot become God.

As we go through some of these lessons dealing with nature, we want to confirm that our children have a right understanding of who God is and how he created all of nature.

For the Family
Enjoying the Lesson Together

Scripture: John 15:1-17, Psalm 139:1-18, 23-24
(remember to choose a verse as your family memory verse with each lesson)

Object Lesson: Play hide and seek outside or inside.

Read Psalm 139:1-18, 23-24

Did you have fun playing hide and seek? You found some good hiding places.

Can we play hide and seek with God? Why not?

Does he play hide and seek with us? He is always with us, isn't he?

God tells us in Psalms 139 that we cannot go anywhere that is away from him. Wherever we go, he is there, always. He remains with us.

In John 15:1-5 we see that we are also to remain with him. Abide, our word for today, means to remain, to stay with. We are always to stay with God and let him work in and through our lives.

Psalm 139 depicts a type of hide and seek game that God uses to explain that we cannot go away from him, and in John 15 he uses grape vines to explain how much we need him.

(If you can visit a vineyard, that would be wonderful, but below is a picture to help explain the verses).

branch

vine

The branches on a vine are very small. All the nutrients for creating fruit come from the vine. The branches are so weak they cannot even hold up the fruit. Most vine dressers use wire or tie up the branches in some way to allow the heavy grapes to hang without touching the ground. It shows us how much the branches rely on the vine to live and to bear fruit. Without the vine, branches dry up and die quickly.

Prayer/Song/Poem: On YouTube you'll find several songs about the vine and branches. Some are excellent. It will take a few minutes to find the better ones. Slugs and Bugs has a good one that is easy for young children.

Ellie Holcomb has a song called "Where Can I Go" about Psalm 139 that is nice.

Activity: Grapes Bible Verse Picture

Make a 3-D grape vine and write verse 5 or one of the other verses from John 15 on the page.

Purple tissue paper or crepe paper cut into sections to wad up and create grapes (about 10 15-inch-long strips of crepe paper or a 5X6 rectangle of tissue paper)

Dark green paper to cut out two leaves

2 Green pipe cleaners

Glue — hot glue or glue dots

Colored printer paper or construction paper — blue, green, or yellow for the background

Instructions:
1. Wad up the purple crepe or tissue paper to create 10 grapes
2. Make a T with the pipe cleaners, then mold them to resemble a branch and stem
3. Cut out two three-pronged leaves out of the green paper
4. Glue down the vine and branch pipe cleaners
5. Under those arrange grapes in a row of 4, row of 3 below that, row of 2 below 3, and one, gluing them under the branch
6. Cut out two leaves and glue them to the top of the grape cluster
7. Under the cluster write your memory verse from John 15.

Picture Books: *Near* and *Known* by Sally Lloyd Jones, *Wonderfully Made* by Krystena Lee; *God Is Always with Me* by Dandi Daley Mackall

Trust

For Mom and Dad
Preparing our Hearts

Scripture: Psalm 115:11; Proverbs 3:5-6; Psalm 118:8-9; Philippians 4:6; Isaiah 55:8; Judges 17:6, 21:25

When we were young in our marriage and young in the ministry, money was so tight. It was tight through most of our ministry, but when you're only part time and going to school, it's really tight. I put Dave through school with my little jobs, and we hardly saw each other. I worked during the day while he went to school, and I went to school at night while he worked. We saw each other for a few minutes each day. During those days, each time things seemed hopeless financially, I found myself plotting, planning, and trying to figure out how to make ends meet. Honestly, I prayed, but I didn't really trust God. I didn't pray and ask God for wisdom or to help us know what to do. I would ask for his help, but then I tried to figure it out myself. It was not good. It was not trust in God. It was lip service to God but trust in myself.

We use the word *trust* from day one of following Jesus; however, as we get older the temptation is to trust more in ourselves and less in God. When we become parents, we are tempted to worry, try to solve our own problems, and make decisions that seem right to us. Most of us pray. Most of us want God's help, but we are either impatient or too worried to even notice what God is doing.

We don't have to live that way. We can truly walk in faith and trust.

One time, our financial situation was so bad, Dave went to pray, and he told God he was not getting up until he heard from him and knew what to do. It was the best thing Dave could have done. He prayed for 45 minutes before anything happened. He just poured his heart out to God. Then, after 45 minutes, he said it was like he was sitting at the feet of Jesus with his head on his lap. He felt God's presence and then he understood God's perspective on our situation. That was a life-changing encounter with God, and it changed our whole family. God assured us that he was in control. He was teaching us to truly trust him. His ways are not our ways. It was still a rough road to walk, but God did provide not long after that in an unexpected way.

Dear, dear friend, I can share this with you with total conviction — we can always trust God. He will always care for us, even when we must walk through hard times, dark times, or painful times, he is always with us. He meets our every need. He strengthens us when we have nothing left to give. God is faithful. We can always pour out our hearts to him. We can bring our fears to him. We can bring our complaints to him. We can trust him with all our feelings, all our circumstances, and all our doubts.

In all things, we can absolutely trust God.

Prayer: If you are struggling right now with worry or fear or difficulties, spend time this week in prayer. Wait on the Lord and ask him to show you his heart and his plan. We can pray that our trust in God is renewed each day and even in this moment.

Preparing to Parent

How do we teach our children to trust God especially when we know we struggle with it ourselves sometimes? His ways don't always make sense to us. Often, like in Judges, we want to do what seems right in our own eyes instead of trusting God's ways.

Truly, our children probably trust God more easily than we do. They don't struggle with worry like we do usually. They don't try to fix everything in their own strength. In this lesson, we may actually be learning from them more than they are learning from us!

As we prepare for this lesson and prepare to talk about trusting God, depending on the age of your children, you may want to be honest that sometimes you struggle, and you know that's wrong. However, one point we definitely want our children to understand in this lesson is that we trust God with them. We have put their lives in God's hands and want them to always follow and trust God. It is the best thing we could ever do for them as their parents.

If you have pictures of a baby dedication you had when they were born or something the church gave you if that is part of your tradition, you can show it to them and talk about how from the beginning you trusted God and thanked God for them.

You may want to pray together acknowledging the goodness of God and how you trust him to take care of each member of your family.

For the Family
Enjoying the Lesson Together

Scripture: Psalm 115:11; Proverbs 3:5-6; Psalm 118:8-9; Psalm 31:14
(remember to choose a verse as your family memory verse with each lesson)

Object Lessons: The Chair Lesson and Do You Trust Me?

Everyone sits down at the table.

You just sat down in your chair. How did you know it would hold you up? How did you know it wouldn't be like Baby Bear's chair when Goldilocks sat in it, and it broke to pieces?

We use faith and trust all the time. We don't even think about it. When you come to dinner, you sit in a chair and gladly eat the wonderful food God has provided, and someone has cooked for you. When you go to sleep at night, you jump into your bed and snuggle into the covers knowing God is watching over you and that your family is with you.

Faith helps you trust that the chair will hold you up, the food will nourish your body, and that God and your family will take care of you.

A second object lesson is easy and fun. Actually, there are several object lessons about trust using the science of surface tension, but this one requires less preparation.

Supplies needed:
Ziploc baggie
Sharpened pencils
Water

Fill the baggie with water and seal it.

Ask your children if they trust you.

Then ask one child if he or she trusts you to hold that bag over his/her head. Tell them, I don't want you to get wet. So, do you trust me to hold a bag of water over your head?

Hold it over his/her head and pick up a pencil.

Ask would you trust me if I poked a pencil through this bag and put it over your head? Remember, I don't want you to get wet. Do you trust me?

Do you think you'll get wet?

Poke the pencil straight through the bag with the pencil sticking out the other side.

No water should leak out as long as the pencil goes in straight.

Go to the next child and ask the same thing, then poke a second pencil through the bag. You should be able to repeat this several times without any water leaks.

You can explain that the bag's material automatically seals the opening around the pencil to prevent water from leaking out. It's the way the polymer is made.

We trust God. He knows things we don't. We trust him because he knows everything! He is wiser, smarter, and more powerful than anyone, and he loves us more than anyone.

Sometimes in the Bible God asks us to do things that don't make sense to us. For instance, he says to love our enemies. He says the first will be last and last will be first. He says the greatest will be least.

It may have seemed silly for me to want to put a bag of water over your head. And it was even sillier for me to want to poke a pencil through the bag. Why do you think I did that? That's right, to teach you about trust (and about polymer plastic). I knew something you didn't know yet. But you trusted me because you know me.

We trust God because we know him and that he loves us. His plans are good, and even when hard times happen or sad things happen, God is always with us, and he will always help us. We can trust him.

Prayer/Song/Poem: Is there an area you have trouble trusting God in or something you worry about? Let's pray about it.

Activity: Play Janga.

As we played the game, we would try to move the block we trusted was safe to move. Sometimes we were right and sometimes we were wrong. Trust is that way too. Sometimes we trust someone to keep their promise, but they break their promise. Other times we trust ourselves, and we fail. Who can we always trust knowing he will never fail? Where can we find truth that is never wrong?

Picture Books: *This I Know* by Clay Anderson, *Quinn's Promise Rock* by Christie Thomas, *The Storm that Stopped* by Alison Mitchell

Walk

For Mom and Dad
Preparing our Hearts

Scripture: Ephesians 5:15-17; Psalm 95:7; Micah 6:8; Psalm 89:15; John 8:12, 12:35; Psalm 119:105

When I was in college, I was a summer missionary in the North Bay in California for ten weeks. One week, at a children's camp, I did a skit around the campfire. That skit has stuck with me probably more than it ever affected any of those watching it. In the darkness, I stood there holding a flashlight. My character cried out to God about how I didn't know how to follow him. I couldn't see where I was going. The other actor played God's voice coming from the dark, and he responded that I should trust him and follow him. Again, I said I couldn't see where I was going. He repeats, "You can't see anything?" I admit I can see enough for one step where the flashlight fell on the path in front of me, and he says, "So?" And I say, "So, I should take that one step?" When I did, of course, the flashlight showed the next step and the next.

This simple skit taught me to walk with God even when I only know enough to take one more step. I trust God and know he will show me the next step in his timing.

In our walk with God, we have many times of uncertainty. We may only see enough or know enough for one more step. Or God may keep us in a holding pattern for a time while he is teaching us. When we find ourselves waiting, our response should be prayer and diving into God's word. Our temptation is to be impatient and even complain. I hope we can remember that God knows his plan, and he will guide us in his time. He knows what is best.

Our walk is not a constant, non-stop moving, but a daily trusting and obeying. Sometimes it is like Genesis 3:8 when God walked with Adam and Eve in the cool of the evening. It's like a nice, evening stroll filled with peace and contentment. Other times our walk is filled with faith and challenges like Abraham when he left his home to go where God would lead. And other times, we may have the hardest walk of all—when God confronts our sin or misunderstanding, and we are brought to our knees. To start walking again may require the help of others around us like Saul needed after the confrontation on the Road to Damascus.

In all of these, we must walk in the light by faith knowing that Jesus knows the way even when we don't.

Prayer: Where are you in your walk? We can pray about that today. Pray for God's assurance and guidance. Pray for peace and contentment. Repent of complaining and fear. God is good, and he promises to always show us the way.

Preparing to Parent

Jesus tells us "Be careful how you walk" and tells us to love mercy and walk humbly. As a family, we can also instill in our children a sense of walking in a way worthy of our family name. Especially as they get older this will be important; however, we need to build this sense of belonging and identity early.

How does Jesus want us to walk? How do we want our family's walk to reflect Jesus? What values do we reveal by the way we walk?

Tackle some of these questions together as a family and begin to develop this sense of identity for your family, a kind of high expectation for behavior and attitude that helps each person identify that they belong.

We, as parents, need to also keep these values in mind. Are we reflecting the values we say are important, or are we only teaching our children in word alone? As we hear many say, we need to walk the walk, not just talk the talk. It's trite, but true.

For the Family
Enjoying the Lesson Together

Scripture: Ephesians 5:15-17; Psalm 95:7; Micah 6:8
(remember to choose a verse as your family memory verse with each lesson)

Object Lesson: Flashlight and Magnifying Glass

This lesson takes a little preparation ahead of time if you want to make it even more exciting. If you don't have time for that, you can make it a nature, exploration walk. However, if you have time, create a walk with signs telling your children which way to go and end up at a destination like a fire pit or a snack at a table or a picnic.

Each child should have a flashlight and a magnifying glass. If you want to make a map for them to follow, you can do that too, but mostly, we want them to find the signs showing them which way to walk and recognize that we follow the things we focus on most. With the magnifying glass, maybe they can follow a bug for a while and see what happens and how they may need to back track to get back on the path. When they are in the shadows, the flashlight will show them the way and they can walk in the light.

You may want to share something like the skit I mentioned in the devotion where God shows us enough for one step sometimes. Even when there's only enough light for one step, we take that one step and obey.

When they get to their destination, celebrate how well they did and let them talk about the challenges. Then, talk about the verses especially Psalm 89:15.

Prayer/Song/Poem: Mary Rice Hopkins has a great song called "Walk Like Jesus" that is on YouTube and is a fun song to teach your children.

Activity: A Path for Parents or Nighttime Adventure

Let the children create a path for the parents to follow. Or go on a flashlight and magnifying glass treasure hunt at dusk and see what bugs and creatures you can find.

Picture Books: *I Walk with Vanessa* by Kerascoet, *Flashlight* by Lizi Boyd, *Candle Walk* by Karin Holsinger Sherman

Obey

For Mom & Dad
Preparing Our Hearts

Scripture: Colossians 1:9-14

I'm always so fascinated by how God works in our lives. Every single time he has called us to go somewhere, he has changed our desires to align with his plan. I remember the night I decided to stay for evening worship while I was home for the weekend from college. I usually drove back to campus after lunch on Sundays so I wouldn't be driving late at night. But I felt like I should stay, so I did. That night, our church invited us to sign up to join a mission trip to the Philippines. I wasn't very adventurous, and I had never thought of going to Asia. At that point in my life, I had never even been on an airplane, didn't have a passport, and was a broke college student, but my heart was beating out of my chest at the thought of this opportunity. I knew God was calling me to go on this trip. As frightening as the idea seemed to me at first, I began to get so excited about going. My desires completely changed to want to obey Christ with every fiber of my being. My love for Christ prompted me to obey. He changed my desires to match his plan. Even though I knew participating in the mission trip would not make God love me any more than he already did, I was so excited to obey him.

First Samuel 15:22 tells us: "To obey is better than sacrifice," meaning God loves our obedience, and our obedience shows our love for him. However, we are not working toward being good enough. We aren't obeying God to earn his favor. Grace alone saves us (Ephesians 2:8-9).

The good works and obedience are fruit of our faith. They show that we are his and that he is truly our God and Savior (Colossians 1:9-14).

I know we know this. I know we say we are saved by grace through faith in Christ. However, we don't always live like that's what we believe. Rather than joyfully serving God out of an overflow and outflow of his love in our lives, we seem to strive and push ourselves to get more and more done. We sometimes seem to try to be super parents or super Christians. Not always, the opposite can also be true, but most faithful followers of Christ often seem to be trying so hard, like we are trying to win God's favor. Obedience is an act of worship, not an act of gaining brownie points.

I try to bring my thinking into a right place when I find myself striving, bargaining, or worrying in my relationship with God, but I don't feel too bad about struggling in this area. I think that's because I comfort myself realizing I'm in good company. The Disciples struggled this way too while walking with Jesus—always wondering who was going to be the greatest in the kingdom and all that. However, we don't see that behavior as much after they received the Holy Spirit. So, I think if we rely on the Holy Spirit and listen to His wisdom, we might stay on track more.

Obedience is our opportunity to show our love and joy in following Christ. It is the opportunity to show the world that he has changed us, and we are his.

Songs: "Teach Me to Obey" from Upper Room Sessions — Bria Jean, "Yes (Obedience)" from Integrity Music, and "Your Will Be Done" by CityAlight

Prayer: If you struggle with a works mentality or getting caught up too much in the "doing" rather than worshipping and following God, then ask Him to help you in this area. Ask Him to help you not pass on this type of attitude to your children or others you disciple. It's easy to do. We need God's help to follow Him well.

Preparing to Parent

While helping our children learn obedience, we as parents are learning to let go little by little. As our children demonstrate their maturity, self-discipline, and obedience, we begin to give them more freedom. When it is done well, our children learn to be independent adults and learn to follow Christ out of the discipline of their hearts rather than living vicariously through our faith and never developing their own relationship with God. This requires God's wisdom and leadership in our parenting and discipling. It requires discernment. And it requires treating each child individually. Some may not be ready for more responsibility at the same age as a sibling.

Proverbs 22:6 has this type of parenting in mind as well as verses like 1 Corinthians 13:11 that call us to maturity. If our focus as parents is to raise independent, wise, godly adults rather than just raising well-behaved children, we will do the painful work of trying to be wise in letting go little by little. It is not easy. A part of us will always wish we could hold our kids in our arms and protect them from the world. But they are not called to stay in our arms. God is calling them to a world for "such a time as this" (Esther 4:14). He has a plan, a purpose, and works He prepared for them before they were born (Ephesians 2:10). We must not stand in their way—in His way.

If we can teach our children that with freedom comes responsibility, and we let them know that as they grow up and mature, we will do our best to give them more freedom and responsibility; hopefully, they will embrace that and look forward to it.

For example: When our children are little, we walk with them as they ride their tricycle or bike with training wheels.

Then, somewhere around 4th grade maybe, we feel they've mastered their bicycle riding and can begin to ride on their own in the neighborhood. Maybe they can ride around the block with friends at some point.

A few years after that, maybe we and the kids can ride our bikes to town, to the park, or to the local fast-food restaurant. Knowing traffic laws and being alert requires maturity.

Then, when they are 16 or later, we start helping them to learn to drive a car.

Similarly, we do the same with instructing them. While they are little, we teach them constantly what is safe and what is not. We tell them yes and no and maybe. We put them in playpens and highchairs where they can't just wander around on their own.

Little by little we stop telling them everything to do, especially as they show their own responsible behaviors and do what they know they should do without being told.

Then, as they get into young adulthood, they may ask our advice, and we share it gladly, but now, they may take it or leave it. It is not an insult but a sign they truly are adults. They respect us enough to ask, but they must make their own grown-up decisions.

I remember the first time my father-in-law said, "I can tell you what I think, but you have to make your own decision." We felt respected, and our respect for him just grew stronger.

I always hold on to the promise from God that if we lack wisdom, all we have to do is ask, and I ask a lot! (James 1:5) May He bless you as you walk this wonderful but challenging road.

Here are some songs that come to mind in this discussion, and if you haven't heard them before, just know all three will make any mommy or daddy cry (especially the daddies). But they are beautiful. Mark Schultz's "He's My Son," Bob Carlisle's "Butterfly Kisses," and Steven Curtis Chapman's "Cinderella."

For the Family
Enjoying the Lesson Together

Scripture: John 14:15, 23; Ephesians 6:1; Colossians 3:20; Matthew 21:28-32
(remember to choose a verse as your family memory verse with each lesson)

Object Lesson: Play a game of Simon Says.

After playing Simon Says, talk about how those who obeyed stayed in the game. Those who didn't, lost the game for that turn. Sometimes when we disobey God or our parents, we have consequences too. Maybe it's a time out or we miss out on something God wanted us to get to do.

Read John 14:15, 23 together.

What does God say about those who obey Him? So, how can we show our love to God?

You can also show your love and respect to your parents when you obey them. Read Ephesians 6:1 and Colossians 3:20. This same kind of verse is found several times in different places in the Bible. Why do you think God would say it so many times? It's important, right? Why is it important for children to obey their parents?

What does it mean to obey God or your parents?

Yes, you do what they say. But how do you do that? Do you do it with a grumpy, whiney attitude?

Do you do it after you finish what you want to do? Do you do it only when you feel like it?

Obedience is doing what you're told without hesitation, arguing, or complaining.

Obeying well is not always easy to do. What could we do if we are having a hard time obeying with joy? We could pray and ask God to help us with our attitude and our "want to."

Another attitude we have to watch out for is where we say, "Yes, I'll do it." But then we don't. We make promises, but we don't follow through. That is not good.

Read Matthew 21:28-32. This story is about people who say they follow Jesus but don't do what He says. Then people who rejected Him at first became followers who obeyed Him. One of the lessons this parable teaches us is that the ones who obey are the ones who truly follow Jesus.

It is not enough to say we want to follow Jesus and obey Him. We must do it.

Prayer/Song/Poem: Children's songs: "Obey" or "I Obey Right Away"

Activity: Cook a recipe together.

Have two teams Team 1 makes up their own recipe and team 2 follows the recipe precisely. I recommend baking cookies or something that requires specific ingredients to turn out well. (You may want to cut the recipes in half for this activity.)

After making the recipes, have everyone try each one. What were the results? Why didn't both recipes turn out well? Obeying God means following His word, His commands. Just like following the directions of a recipe so things turn out right, when we follow God's directions things turn out the way He plans. When we don't, things can turn out very wrong.

Picture Books: *Library Lion* by Michelle Knudsen, *Sir Maggie the Mighty: A Book About Obedience* by Michael P. Waite

Discern

For Mom and Dad
Preparing Our Hearts

Scripture: 1 John 4:1

One time I attended a worship conference at a church I'd never been to. I knew they had some different beliefs than I did, but they weren't major differences, so I thought it would be a fun conference to attend. Well, it became kind of comical for me. I had a hard time focusing on worship because my discernment was working overtime. One speaker shared, and part of what she shared was straight from scripture. Then, she'd share what I'll call "man's wisdom." Some of it was not outright heresy, but it was not supported by scripture. So, my mind was going back and forth: scripture, man's wisdom, good verse, that's not in the Bible. It was a spiritual ping-pong match in my mind. The whole conference was that way for me, and I did not enjoy it very much in the end. However, I was thankful that the Holy Spirit was helping me to test the teaching, hold on to the truth, and not become confused or deceived.

Discernment, like wisdom, is an essential part of the Christian life for every believer. God does give some the gift of discernment, and that gift is stronger in people who have been given that gift. However, many of the gifts are also characteristics we are to demonstrate in our walk with God. Discernment is one of those.

Psalm 119:125 talks of discernment helping us understand God's word.

Proverbs 28:11 talks about seeing through the ignorance of people who think they are wise but aren't.

Hosea 14:9 talks of those with discernment listening carefully and following God faithfully.

Today, in our culture, everyone seems to think they know the truth. The division we are experiencing politically and religiously results from too many of us sharing what we think is right instead of really discerning Truth through God's word and his wisdom. And even when we do understand and discern the Truth, the world will not understand it and will call it foolish. 1 Corinthians 2:14 reminds us of that. "The person without the Spirit does not accept the things that come from the Spirit of God but considers them foolishness and cannot understand them because they are discerned only through the Spirit." (NIV) But God wants us to be wise and discerning, nonetheless. What a blessing to realize the Holy Spirit will give us understanding. We can humbly walk in wisdom and truth because the Holy Spirit gives us discernment to understand. We can walk faithfully as disciples of Christ and guide our children as well because of this blessing. We must not squander it.

Discernment is mostly paying attention, using the wisdom God gives us, and also listening to our conscience when something doesn't seem right. This is important when we listen to teachers, especially Bible teachers and those who tell us how to raise our children. In Proverbs 8:12, Wisdom is speaking saying she lives together with good judgment and knows where to find knowledge and discernment. We just need God's wisdom to live this life and to parent as we should.

Discernment is wisdom at work, helping us understand what is not necessarily obvious on the surface. It helps us know what may be hidden so that we can protect ourselves and our children.

One example from my early days of parenting was when I was reading a book someone gave me on how to parent an infant. I read it, and throughout the book, I kept thinking, "This is not right!" It was saying that my child was manipulating me when she cried, and from day one, I should have her on a schedule. This felt very wrong to me, and I talked to my midwife. She was shocked someone gave me that book, and she told me to ignore it. She had seen many infants become dehydrated from this practice, and then she told me the author was not even a parent or someone who knew anything about raising children. He wasn't even married. That author was Bill Gothard, the founder of the Institute in Basic Youth Conflicts that has come under such disrepute.

The Holy Spirit gives us insight if we just listen. He helps us know what we need to know as we navigate this life. We are not alone. We are not without guidance. Praise God for giving us the Holy Spirit to guide and comfort us along the way.

Our prayer should be, like Job's, "The ear tests the words it hears just as the mouth distinguishes between foods. So let us discern for ourselves what is right; let us learn together what is good." (Job 34:3-4, NLT)

Prayer: Pray for listening ears to hear what the Holy Spirit is guiding us to do. Pray for discernment, wisdom, understanding, and knowledge so that we can be the disciples of Christ we are meant to be, serving God well, guiding our children well, and helping build the kingdom of God, bringing glory to our wonderful God.

Preparing to Parent

Many times, God has given our children the ability to discern things better than we do as adults. We sometimes assume they are just being silly or are trying to get out of something they don't want to do like going to bed or hugging someone goodbye. In reality, sometimes they are discerning something we are missing.

Today with so many reports of abuse, most of us don't force out children to hug someone they don't feel comfortable hugging. When it comes to other issues, it's not as easy. Recognizing that our child may be discerning something spiritual is sometimes difficult. We need to ask God to open our eyes and help us discern if there is something that needs to be dealt with. If nothing else, we can pray with our children and assure them they are safe while acknowledging their feelings.

However, please do not discount our enemy. He does not care if he hurts an innocent child or a seasoned sinner. He wants to steal, kill, and destroy. So, we should take the fact that he is evil personified seriously. That does not mean we walk in fear or worry. Our God is greater, and the Holy Spirit helps us know what we need to know if we will listen.

When our children are old enough, we need to talk to them seriously about the enemy's lies, but we always need to make sure they know that God is greater, and if we belong to God, Satan cannot have us. It seems we walk a fine line in this area of our faith. If we focus too much on Satan, we lose focus on God and doing what we're called to do. However, if we ignore or try to bargain with the enemy, we can make terrible mistakes. Our focus, strength, purpose, and actions are all to bring God glory and obey Him. We simply must be aware of the enemy and his lies so that we are not taken in. Discernment is the key.

Scripture: Psalm 119:125, 169; Job 34:3-4; Proverbs 3:21, 8:12, 28:11; Hosea 14:9; 1 John 4:1
(remember to choose a verse as your family memory verse with each lesson)

Object Lesson: Discerning with our Senses

Items needed:
Sleeping masks for each child or blindfolds
Different fruits cut up and in opaque containers
Small items they can touch and recognize without seeing them

Each child puts on a sleeping mask or blindfold, and you will have them taste a bite of fruit to see if they can discern what the fruit is. Take several turns, and then switch to touching the small items and see if they can guess what they are.

Afterwards talk about how they could tell what each thing was, or if they had trouble, talk about why it was difficult.

When we are discerning, we can't always see clearly what is true. We must pray and discern what is true. Sometimes the Holy Spirit will warn us that we are about to make a bad choice or get into trouble. Or maybe someone says something, and we discern it is not true because it goes against what the Bible says. We can discern the truth in situations even when we cannot see everything with our eyes, but the Holy Spirit tells us the truth.

Prayer/Song/Poem: We can help our children pray for wisdom and discernment.

The songs "I Will Trust You God" and "I Might Be Small" by Allstars Kids Club is a nice kids' song that has a good message that goes along with this lesson when talking about God being stronger than everything.

Activity: Treasure hunt with scriptures

Print cards/clues that help children find the next card/clue

1. Give them: Proverbs 3:21-22

2. On a necklace: Proverbs 8:18-19

3. In a bowl with fruit or in the fruit drawer of the fridge: Hosea 14:9

4. Found on the front walkway/path to the house: Proverbs 8:10-11

5. Found in a wallet or purse: Proverbs 8:33-34

6. Found on a gate or doorway: Psalm 119:103

7. Found under honey container or in the sugar bowl: Job 34:3-4

8. Found in the refrigerator or pantry between two types of food: Proverbs 8:12
   For a prize in finding all the clues, give each child a compass to remind them that God's word helps them find wisdom and right way to go, and discernment to know the truth.

Picture Books: *What Is Truth* by Elizabeth Urbanowicz, *The Oak Inside the Acorn* by Max Lucado

A book for parents: *All That's Good* by Hannah Anderson

Avoid

For Mom & Dad:
Preparing Our Hearts

Scripture: 1 Corinthians 10:13, Galatians 5:16-17, 1 Timothy 6:11, James 4:7, Proverbs 16:17

I'm very happy to say I have never had poison ivy. From those I've known who have had it, I feel very blessed. But I have one friend who is so allergic to poison ivy, she cannot be outside in an area where it grows because the wind blowing the molecules her way causes her to break out as though she'd rolled around in it and even swallowed some of it. Horrible! But it got me to thinking about avoiding evil. Sometimes we just get in the vicinity of others doing something that tempts us, and before we know it, it is like we've jumped right into the middle of it all. Gossip, lust, rebellion, or any other temptation can cause a bad case of sin. We are so susceptible to sin.

"Avoid evil." Proverbs 16:17 in the ERV uses those words. We are reminded in verses like these that temptation, or at least our choice to follow temptation, is just that: a choice. We can avoid evil. We can avoid falling into sin. But avoidance is a decision we need to make before we are tempted. God promises that He always provides a way out of temptation. If we take this seriously, we are going to avoid temptation as much as possible, and if a temptation surprises us, we look for that way out.

That is the first way to avoid temptation and sin. We literally avoid temptation. If we know something is a temptation or weakness for us, we don't entertain the thoughts that lead us into it, we don't go to that place that causes us to stumble, and we don't put ourselves into a situation that we know will play into our temptation. A simple example my husband often shares is how he used to drive to work past a donut shop. Every day, he just couldn't resist. He would stop and get a couple donuts which he knew he did not need. The only way he found to break that temptation and that choice to stop was to change the route he drove to work each day. It was a simple change, but it worked.

A second way we avoid temptation and sin is in the battlefield of our minds. 2 Corinthians 10:5 teaches us to "destroy" ideas that tempt us and take every thought captive making it obey Christ. Our hearts and minds are deceitful (Jeremiah 17:9). We can rationalize anything. I'm always amazed at how creative we can be when we do that. We are very creative. That's why 2 Cor. 10:5 is so important.

The third way to avoid temptation and sin is confession. James 5:16 tells us God heals us when we do. We've found that confession releases the hold temptation has on us. It sets us free from guilt and shame, and it heals our minds of the temptation.

The fourth way is scripture memory. Psalm 119:11 reminds us that hiding God's word in our hearts strengthens us to fight against sin.

A fifth way we also find is being grateful and joyful. The Bible teaches that the joy of the Lord is our strength (Nehemiah 8:10). It also shows us that the Lord is our strength which results in joy. When we recognize God's lordship and help in our lives, we find gratitude, praise, and joy in that, and in all of it, we find strength to live a victorious Christian life. (Psalm 28:7)

As with everything in our Christian Walk, we model for our children how to walk with Christ. We tend to hide our temptations and weaknesses from our children, and some of that may be appropriate. However, what about when we lose our temper in front of our children or worry about bills? We can confess that we struggle at times, and then we can share how we deal with sin and temptation in our own lives.

Prayer: The first thing we need to do is confess our sin. We can ask for forgiveness and wisdom. We need both so we can walk faithfully with our God. We need to spend time in praise and worship as well. The following two songs may help usher us into a time of worship.

You may find Alisa Childers' songs "Prone to Wander" and "The Battle Is the Lord's" encouraging as you think about and pray about sin and temptation in your life. These songs are so full of truth and scripture. Also, her song "Pray for Me" is about facing temptation and standing strong in our walk with God and committing to pray for each other. This would be a beautiful song for a husband and wife to commit to for each other.

Preparing to Parent

One of the truths we want our children to understand, especially when discussing sin, is that God warns us about things that will hurt us. It is His kindness that calls us to repentance. You may want to share the story of Adam and Eve when they first chose to sin. In addition to just sharing the story, we can see the kindness of God in His reaction to their hiding and blaming. Yes, there were consequences for the sin, just like He warned them there would be. However, He clothed them and blessed them with children. He didn't accuse them or torment them. He simply confronted them. I always find the simple question, "Who told you that you were naked?" reveals how accusing Satan is. He tempts us to sin, and when we choose to give in, he accuses and shames us for what we did. God doesn't do that.

The world through mythical stories and even just the way people talk about God create a picture of a god waiting to zap everyone — to smite them — as soon as they mess up. We know the True God is not like that, and our children need to have the right understanding of God as a holy God who loves them and wants to help them live a life close to Him.

We must be careful, however, not to paint the other incorrect picture of God — that He is a benign all-loving God who says everything is okay. God hates sin and what it does to us. He does not tolerate rebellion and stubborn disobedience. He is not mocked.

God is always ready to forgive and restore us to a right relationship with Him, but just like Adam and Eve had to leave the garden, all sin has consequences. We must help our children gain an accurate understanding of God as loving, gentle, patient, and forgiving but learning to respect Him because He is also holy, perfect, and truthful.

For the Family
Enjoying the Lesson Together

Scripture: 1 Timothy 6:11, James 4:7, Proverbs 16:17
(remember to choose a verse as your family memory verse with each lesson)

Object Lesson: Poisonous Plants or Cacti

Because we love our children, we warn them about things that might hurt them, like a hot pan on the stove. Because God loves us, He warns us that sin will hurt us.

Find poison ivy, thorn bushes, poison oak, cacti, or other plants that should be avoided. You will talk about how everyone should avoid these plants and why. Then share what happens if they don't listen to what you said and don't avoid them.

If you've ever had poison ivy or poison oak, share what it was like in hilarious detail. Make it fun, if possible, but help them realize it was not actually fun. It was miserable. Talk about how funny you looked to everyone with pink spots of calamine lotion on, but that you were miserable.

I share about the time I saw this cute cactus my grandma had on her porch. It looked so soft. I knew it was a cactus, but it didn't look dangerous. So, I carefully, barely touched it to see if it was as soft as it looked. Guess what. It wasn't! I got several spines in my finger, and they hurt! They weren't just prickly, but they had little hooks on them, so they hurt going in and coming out. I never touched another cactus again!

Proverbs 16:17 says that our path should lead us away from evil so we can stay safe. We stay on the path so that we don't get poison ivy/thorns. We do the same in our walk with God.

What happens when we choose to ignore God's warnings and do what He says not to do? What is that called? Sin, that's right. God tells us to avoid situations and people who might cause us to go against God's warnings. He says He will always give us a way to escape from sin (1 Corinthians 10:13).

If you know something tempts you to make the wrong choices, what can you do to avoid it? Let's say you know Mom hides cookies in her nightstand. Mom has told you not to eat any cookies or sweets before dinner. Can you avoid the temptation to eat a cookie? How? That's right, stay away from the nightstand. Don't even go into Mom and Dad's bedroom. Focus on something else. Maybe you could read a book, ask to eat a healthy snack, or play outside. Stay away from the temptation.

Remember Psalm 119:11? When we hide God's word in our hearts, we can also find more strength and determination to avoid the temptations that can lead us the wrong way.

We can also pray for God to help us and protect us. Remember in the Lord's prayer, he said we should ask God to protect us from temptation. Prayer and Bible verses are like fences along the path, so we don't step into the places where the poison ivy/thorns are.

Prayer/Song/Poem: (Sing to the tune of "Jesus Loves Me")
Avoid temptation, choose not to sin
Stay on the path God's leading in
Never wander from left to right
Keep God's word and plan in sight
Because Jesus loves you (3X)
He'll never let you go

Jesus loves me when I'm good
And I do the things I should
Jesus loves me when I'm bad
But it makes Him very sad
Yes, Jesus loves me (3X)
The Bible tells me so.

Activity: Making Bracelets

Supplies needed:
Shrinky dink material
Markers
Either elastic cord for bracelets and beads
Jump rings for the charms you make

Alternate plan:
silicone plain bracelets
Permanent markers

Write scripture references for the verses you've memorized as a family, especially ones that help fight temptation like Psalm 119:11, Proverbs 16:17. Kids can also draw some flowers or other pictures. (It helps if you draw circles for them to draw and write in so they will all be the same size).

Follow the directions to create a hole for making these into charms and bake them according to the directions.

While they bake, create beaded bracelets using elastic cord and colorful beads.

Add charms to jump rings and put them between the beads of the bracelets.

If you want a more masculine choice for boys, you can order plain silicone wristbands/bracelets that you can color and put stickers on. Each child can write a verse on them to remind them of that verse.

If the words wear off with time, have them write a new memory verse on it each time.

This activity is meant to be similar to the Jewish practice of putting scripture on their hands to remind them of the verses.

Picture Books: *Arlo and the Great Big Cover-Up* by Betsy Childs Howard, *Broken: The Problem of Sin* by Floyd Gary Pierce, *Don't Blame the Mud: Only Jesus Makes Us Clean* by Marty Machowski

Rest

For Mom & Dad
Preparing our Hearts

Scripture: Psalm 62:1-7

We were setting up for an event. We do a lot of vendor fairs and homeschool conventions. This event set-up was not going well. First, it was very hot which just made everything a little more difficult. It seemed every step of the set-up process had problems, and we lost a whole bag of screws for putting a backdrop together. It was frustrating. My kids were helping, and they were bickering and hangry. Finally, I just said, "Guys, we're on the same team here. We need to chill out and just tackle this one thing at a time." We all sat down for a minute, drank some water, and waited for their dad to get back with some screws from the store. One of my sons said, "Could it get any worse." I couldn't help it. I laughed. I said, "Yes, it could. We aren't in pain. We aren't sick. We aren't facing a life-threatening situation. We are just hot and tired while setting up, and yes, it's been difficult, but it's not horrible. We need to keep perspective." We all lightened up after that, and in those moments, we felt God's rest even as we worked. We actually had some fun as we finished up with the new screws in hand. God's peace is such a blessing.

In our busy lives, especially as parents, being still and resting seems like the last thing on our list. Being able to rest in the Lord and spend time with Him seems impossible. We know it is important though, so we try.

In addition, living in a culture that is increasingly negative toward Christian beliefs can bring stress and try to steal our peace and rest in Christ.

We must pray for God to help us find calm within the chaos, a stillness in the busyness, and peace in the difficult cultural times. The example of John Wesley's mom is always an encouragement. She had 19 children, and she would sit in her chair putting her apron over her head so she could pray. That was her solace and quiet time with God. Her children respected it, and they never bothered her in those moments. Surely, if she could make time for God in her life, we can too. Psalm 62:1-7 reminds us to wait quietly before God resting in Him, encourages us to find God as our shelter and refuge, and admonishes us to find hope in Him.

The Psalmist speaks of his trust in God and how He knows God will bring victory. When we hold onto that truth, we can find peace in all circumstances, even the lifelong challenge of raising children.

I want to share a personal note here with you, I want so much to help you find this peace. I tried so hard to be the perfect mother, pastor's wife, missionary, and everything else I took on as a title. I was overly busy, always tired, and loved every minute of it despite all that (Yes, I have a bit of a Type A personality). But I have regrets. I regret not using more of my time just being a mom. I regret fretting and stressing about so many things. It took some time of pain and serious discomfort to learn to rest in God no matter what was happening around us, but he has finally helped me learn this lesson. For three years we served in a church that was one of the hardest and most uncomfortable situations we've ever been in. Every day was painful. There were wonderful times as well, but even those were shadowed by the difficulties of the church's situation. Through that difficult time, God taught me to trust, to rest, and to be flexible. I was able to love people who were hateful toward us. And through it all, I found peace. It made no sense, but what a total blessing it has been (Philippians 4:4-7).

The lesson has spilled over into many areas of my life. Helping our children become independent adults has been challenging, but I feel at peace. God is my refuge, and I can go into His presence and pray earnestly for all the decisions and challenges my children face. If I could hand this peace to you, I would. But the only way I know how to do that is to share the verses with you and encourage you to trust those verses and surrender. Pray and trust. God is so good, and He will take care of you.

If I could have walked this kind of peace as a young mom, I wonder what I could have given to my children in their walks with God. I wonder how our ministry could have been different.

Prayer: Take time to pour out your heart to God. Where are you stressed? What worries you? Don't hold back those concerns from God. He knows your heart anyway. He knows your thoughts and where you struggle. He is with you, and He wants to give you peace.

Preparing to Parent
How can we make our homes a place of peace?

Let's face it, if our kids are going through a stage where they fight all the time, this can be especially challenging. I encourage you to step up and deal with it. Don't take it as "just a stage." We may not be able to make them become best friends, but we can set the rules that say every human being deserves respect even when they are your little brother or sister. I was not above threatening to join their hands to each other with yarn for an hour or two until they could speak nicely to one another. Of course, with some children it might be better to insist that they each take a time out until they are ready to say something kind to one another. Either way, we are working to help them change their attitudes and come to a place of being able to show respect even if they aren't ready to show friendship or love to each other. That will come with maturity, hopefully.

The second biggie is if you have tension in your marriage or with your ex. This definitely should become a serious matter of prayer and possibly counseling. We are adults. We should be able to find a way to show respect to one another even when the marriage has failed. If you are married, and there is a lot of tension, pray for wisdom to find the source of that tension and tackle it.

Two things we tell every couple we counsel:
1. Remember you are on the same team. You tackle the problem together, not turn on each other.

2. Every person needs to feel heard and understood. We teach them and practice with them doing what we call a "talk and listen" session. Some people think it's silly to listen and repeat what someone says, but sometimes we need that, and it is shocking when we begin to realize our spouse did not understand what we were saying at all. Once they do hear and understand, we've seen such healing of the relationship. Nothing else may change except that the person feels heard. Sometimes that is enough.

These two are often the biggest issues causing our homes to feel chaotic and not peaceful.

Some other considerations are talking to our children to find out what may be concerning them or stressing them. What is your home like when they come home from going somewhere? How can you appeal to their five senses, creating a special atmosphere of peace?

> Worship music playing softly in the background
> A yummy smell in the kitchen
> A soft place to sit and talk, greeting them with a hug
> Smiling when you see them
> A small snack that they love

Consider how your spouse is greeted when they come home as well.

All of these can help create a peaceful haven in your home.

For the Family
Enjoying the Lesson Together

Scripture: Psalm 16:1-9, Matthew 11:28-29, Psalm 46:10, Psalm 91:4
(remember to choose a verse as your family memory verse with each lesson)

Object Lesson: Resting and Recharging

Dim the lights and read Psalm 16:1-9.

Plug in your cell phone/iPad (or whatever is appropriate for your child). A toy robot would be a great example too as you charge it. Ask why we plug in some things each day. Explain or let the child explain that batteries need to recharge. In a way, our bodies need to recharge. Our minds need to relax. We rest by sleeping.

Isn't it wonderful when you're sleepy to just lie down and snuggle under the covers. You take a deep breath and just relax. You're not worrying about your homework or what you have to do. You just relax. Take a deep breath with me right now. Then, let it out and relax. Doesn't that feel great? It's like we are recharging our batteries for tomorrow.

When the batteries are recharging, our phone/iPad/robot just rests. We don't do the things we usually do with it. It is still.

In Psalms 46:10 God tells us to be still and know that He is God. Sometimes we don't like being still. It's not like God is scolding us, "Be still!" No, He's calling us be still and KNOW He is God. This rest is even bigger and better than sleep that helps our bodies and minds rest and recharge. This rest s for our spirit because nothing is more important than knowing Jesus, His love, and His forgiveness. All day, when doing schoolwork or practicing basketball, we are trying our best, and that is good.

You listen to Mom and me (Dad and me) and work hard to obey. But with God, it's different. No matter how hard we try, we cannot be perfect. We can try and try and try, and we fail. But God says be still. Come to Me and rest. Just rest. Stop trying. Stop struggling. Stop worrying. Just stop. Be still.

Now, know that He is God. He wants us to know He has covered us. We can rest and know that He loves us fully — completely forever. Do you feel how wonderful that is?

Psalm 91:4 says the God covers us with his feathers. He shelters us with his wings. Does God literally have feathers and wings? No, so what picture is this showing us about God?

That's right. He, just like a mama bird covers her baby bird with her wings to protect them and keep the warm and safe, God covers us with His love and protection.

Romans 8:1 says now that we follow Jesus, there is no condemnation. Sometimes we feel like we aren't good enough for God to love us. We know we fail Him and make bad choices. We try and try, but God tells us to rest. Be still. Trust Him. He has covered all our sin and forgives us.

So, tonight and each night, as we get ready to sleep and recharge our bodies and minds, first remember that we can always rest in Jesus and be still knowing He is God and He has us covered.

Prayer/Song/Poem: Read Psalm 23 or Sally Lloyd Jones' book and sing "The Night Song" by CityAlight

Activity: The Wiggles

You may not want to do any activity with this lesson, but if you want to, you could play the wiggle and still game. The leader says, "Wiggle" and everyone has to move until the leader says, "Be still." When the leader says, "Be still" everyone freezes. The first one to move loses, and Mom or Dad may help that happen by tickling someone or making funny faces and making them laugh (although technically that means Mom or Dad lost), but it's good for giggles.

Picture Books: *Found* by Sally Lloyd Jones, *Don't Close Your Eyes* by Bob Hostetler, *Be Still* by Kathryn O'Brien

Remember

For Mom and Dad
Preparing Our Hearts

Scripture: Proverbs 22:6; John 3

Before we came home after seven years overseas, our church surprised us with a slideshow of the work we'd done while there and memories that made us laugh and cry. It was also a tribute to all that God had done in those seven years. Remembering helped us thank God for all he'd done in and through us there. We felt loved and appreciated as we shared those memories together. The pictorial testimony of what God had done was so powerful.

In John 3, John testifies about who Jesus is, and he says that Jesus testifies about what he knows. When people share testimonies, we learn and then remember what God has done. We learn who God is and how he works in and through lives.

If you have never done it, I would encourage you to write out your testimony and even write out a timeline of your spiritual journey. Each of us should share our testimonies of God's work and goodness in our lives with our children. This helps build their faith and it strengthens our own faith as we remember all that Christ has done in our lives.

A simple way to write a testimony is to talk about life before Christ, how you recognized your need for Christ, how you came to Christ, and then what he has done in your life since you chose to follow him.

Too often, people seem to think their testimony is not that powerful or that they need to know a ton of scriptures to make their testimony worthwhile. The truth is, testimonies are our stories of God's work in our lives, and they are very powerful. I've talked with skeptics who mocked my faith and mocked the Bible. Then, they asked why I was a Christian, assuming I was coerced by pushy parents who shamed me into "faith." I simply shared my story of how I came to understand my need for a Savior and how I chose to follow Christ. I shared how it changed my life completely even though I was only seven years old. They could not argue with it, and they stopped mocking and seemed to just think about what I said. I've seen it happen many times. With our children, our testimonies are even more powerful because they know us and how much we love them. We must be honest and share the truth. It changes lives and affects hearts. God uses our stories for his glory.

Prayer: Pray that God reminds you of how he's worked in your life so you can share your stories with your children. Pray that they will be open to and blessed by what you share. Pray for wisdom to know what to share and how to share it.

Preparing to Parent

As we parent our children, we consider when God is opening the door for more than just a teachable moment but a defining moment. These are the times when we encourage our children by telling them what we see God doing in their lives. These go deeper than teachable moments because they help our children begin to see who they are in Christ and how he may want to use their lives.

An example is when we help our children understand that we are their home. No matter where they go, they are loved unconditionally and will always have a place in our hearts and our home. This defines their identity as part of our family forever. It is part of who they are in this world — a part of our family.

Maybe someone is critical of how our child behaved in church, but instead of getting angry at our child, we recognize that their behavior is normal for their age (if it was) and encourage them in how we see that they love church and enjoy meeting people there. Or maybe we see creativity, boldness, generosity, kindness, or gentleness in our children. These attributes are not flattery but are defining how God is working in their lives.

Too often our culture wants us to build up our child's self-esteem. This is contrary to biblical teaching and is usually full of shallow compliments and flattery built on performance, beauty, or even false narratives. Self-esteem teaches our kids to be narcissistic rather than focused on God. It is dangerous and unhealthy.

Defining moments build security, understanding, and purpose in a child's life.

Prayer: We pray for God to open our eyes to these opportunities to bless our children.

For the Family
Enjoying the Lesson Together

Scripture: Luke 22:19; 1 Corinthians 11:24-25; Joshua 4:1-8; Psalm 77:11
(remember to choose a verse as your family memory verse with each lesson)

Object Lesson: Photo albums/baby book

Look through the albums and baby book(s) and talk about memories together.

It is fun remembering what we've done as a family. Jesus wants us to remember what He did for us as well. How can we remember what Jesus did for us?

We have the Bible we can read again and again about what Jesus did.

We can tell others what Jesus has done in our lives. It helps us also remember.

We remember by having the Lord's Supper. This is a special time when we have bread or crackers and grape juice or wine like in the Bible. When we are followers of Jesus, we take the Lord's Supper and remember Jesus' sacrifice on the cross and that He rose again giving us new life.

We can make reminders. What reminder would you make?

In Joshua 4 we read a story about a memorial to help the Israelites remember what God did for them.

Prayer/Song/Poem: "Always Remember" is a beautiful children's song by Angie Killian Music that fits with this lesson beautifully, and Ellie Holcomb's song "Don't Forget to Remember" as well.

Activity: Sticky Notes

Give each child a sticky note pad and pen.

During the week each family member can leave notes on bathroom mirrors or in lunch boxes or on doorways to remind each other a Bible verse, a thank you for what someone has done, or saying what God has done. Little reminders will be everywhere.

If you enjoy crafts, we can create many small crafts that help us remember what Jesus did. An easy and inexpensive one that children from about age 4 and up can do is to make a cross and Resurrection hanging scene out of paper plates.

Supplies Needed:
Cheap paper plates (the thin flimsy kind) (5 per child)
Paint (yellow, orange, black, brown, green, blue)
Stapler and staples or glue dots/glue
Scissors
Yarn
Hole punch

I made a video of this craft on YouTube. You can find it on my channel.

1. Paint one plate orange and yellow like a sunset
2. Paint second plate light blue
3. On the back of the 3rd plate, paint a solid black silhouette of the three crosses
4. On the back of the 4th plate, paint the empty tomb
5. On the 5th plate cut out a circle for the stone and paint it brown and a sun painted yellow
6. Staple or glue the two background plates together back-to-back
7. Staple or glue the crosses to the sunset plate and the empty tomb to the blue sky plate
8. Glue the tomb stone by the empty tomb and sun on the blue sky.
9. Add yarn as a hanger.

Picture Books: *The Garden, the Curtain, and the Cross* by Carl Laferton, *The Promise* by Jason Helopoulos, *I See Jesus See* by Nancy Guthrie, *Why Is There a Cross?* By Kathleen Bostrom, *Don't Forget to Remember* by Ellie Holcomb

Know

For Mom and Dad
Preparing our Hearts

Scripture: John 10:1-5, 27-28; John 8:42-47

When I was around seven years old, after I had become a Christian, we were driving down the highway. I was sitting in the back seat of the car watching out the car window when this insistent voice went off in my head. It was saying over and over, "Open the door, open the door, open the door." Without thinking I reached for the door handle when a small whisper of a voice in my mind said, "Stop." I stopped, and I realized what I was about to do. It was then that I realized Satan doesn't care how old we are. At that point I had enough discernment to recognize it had been Satan's voice trying to hurt me, and God's voice that saved me. Later, I connected it with the verse that tells us Satan wants to kill, steal, and destroy. He is evil personified.

The point is, we are in a battle — Our enemy wants to steal our joy and peace. He wants to destroy our relationships with family and friends. He wants to kill us if he can. And he will do whatever he can to prevent us from following Christ. If we are following Christ, he will try to confuse us and get us to abuse God's word.

We don't need to focus on Satan and make proclamations or anything like that. But we do need to know God's word, it's so imperative! Focusing on hearing God's voice and knowing when he's speaking is vital. We need to take this seriously.

We may need some clarification on this topic because we have those who believe we should pray about every tiny decision and wait for God's still, small voice to guide us, such as what pants to wear today, where to park, and other small everyday decisions. There are others who believe if we say God spoke to us, we are trying to add to scriptures, like God has given us a revelation beyond scripture. Both of these ideas are flawed. The Bible speaks of people living their lives, even getting married and doing all the things we do in work and family and just walking as people of faith, not necessarily praying about every little thing. It never tells us to pray about each little decision and to wait for an answer. However, we may have times when we're getting ready for our day and sense a strong prompting from the Holy Spirit to add something to our bag as we're leaving the house. We have no idea why, but we obey that prompting. Then, to our surprise, God uses that item during our day — either we needed it unexpectedly or someone else did. That is God speaking to us. Other times, we may be praying about something and a verse pops into our head. I guess some could argue that wasn't God speaking; it was just that we have God's word in our hearts and remembered it, but I believe it is God's Spirit speaking to us and comforting us, bringing it back to the forefront of our memory.

We must be aware of abuses and when some misguided people use "words from the Lord" to manipulate others. We need to use discernment and the word of God. God will not contradict his word. He will not call us to do something contrary to what he's taught us in scripture. We are good at justifying our choices and desires. We must be careful not to abuse God speaking as an excuse to just do what we want or what seems right in our own eyes.

That why our word for this week is "know." We must know God's voice. We must know God's word. We do not want to be fooled by false teachers, by the enemy's lies, or by our own rationalizations. We want to know the truth and follow the truth. We want to obey God's voice.

The world likes to make fun of Christians implying that we hear voices like someone with mental issues. However, we know the truth, and the truth is, the Holy Spirit speaks to us often if we will just listen. He reminds us of scriptures we know that help us in different situations. He reminds us of what God has already done in our lives so we can be strengthened in the present circumstance. We need to thank God that he speaks to us and is not silent.

Prayer: We must pray for wisdom and discernment so we are faithful to know and apply God's word correctly, and so we can easily recognize which voice is speaking to our hearts.

Preparing to Parent

As parents, we are sometimes a little concerned about talking about hearing God's voice because we think our children will misunderstand or expect God to speak audibly to them. However, once they are believers, they need to know this is a normal part of our walk with God. They need to be able to distinguish God's voice from their own and from the enemy's voice.

One way that helped when I was young was learning that Satan's voice is always pushy, impatient, ad negative. God's voice is always patient, and even when he is correcting us, he does no injury — he doesn't tear us down, but he extends hope and forgiveness. Often the voice that we consider our own voice that says mean things about us to ourselves is really Satan's voice disguised as our own. Satan's lies extend the other way as well. We are told by our culture and by some churches that we are okay, we are enough. We are encouraged to say affirmations, claiming the truth of our identities in Christ. At the core of these sentiments is usually a self-focused Gospel that tries to placate and flatter our egos. Satan will either get us to ignore God's word or abuse God's word. These fluffy, feel-good "Christians" are often the enemy's tools in disguise as they lead us away from God's word to an abuse of his holiness and call to repentance.

Check for understanding as you talk about all this with your child. And remind them repeatedly that God's voice is first found in the Bible. We may hear him speak when we pray, and often when we hear God's voice, it is the Holy Spirit reminding us of Bible verses we've read or memorized. It's not something weird or spooky. It's God working in our lives to help us become closer to him and to do what he wants us to do. We should remind children that God will never oppose his Word. We can check for understanding on this point by asking questions like: "Would God tell you to take something that isn't yours?" "Would God tell you to be friends with someone other kids don't like?" "Would God tell you to give your last bit of money to help with a missions trip your church is planning?" "Would God tell you to lie to your mom?" God will not tell us to do something that is against what the Bible says.

For the Family
Enjoying the Lesson Together

Scripture: John 10:1-5, 27-28
(remember to choose a verse as your family memory verse with each lesson)

Object Lesson: Who's Talking

You can arrange this ahead of time or just do it off the cuff. You will call someone your child knows and let them hear the person talk on speaker phone. Have the child who recognizes the voice first say the person's name and hello.

After a few, call a friend of yours or a friend that only one child might know better than the others. Ask why only one child recognized that voice — because it was her friend or because they know the person better.

We recognize the voices of those we know.

Read the scripture.

This says that those who know Jesus, know his voice and follow him. How can we know Jesus' voice?

By knowing the Bible

The Bible is God's word, which means it reflects his voice. So, when we hear something in our mind and spirit, we can know if it is God reminding us or telling us to do something or if it is our own voice or the voice of the enemy trying to confuse us.

Read John 15:9; Hebrews 13:5

What do you notice about God's voice? What does he say to us in these verses? If you hear a voice in your head that says, "God could never forgive you for what you did. You are terrible." Would that be God's voice?

God's voice will always say the truth and will never say the opposite of the Bible.

Prayer/Song/Poem: Learn the song by the Gettys called "Speak O Lord" and sing it together. Several groups have a memory verse song for John 10:27.

Activity: Share memory verses.

How many verses has your family memorized? Keep a tally and celebrate that you've hidden God's word in your hearts, and you know God's voice from knowing his word.

Picture Books: *Chasing God's Glory* by Dorina Lazo Gilmore-Young, *His Sheep Hear His Voice* by Kathy Doerscher, *Little Ewe* by Laura Sassi

Love (God)

For Mom and Dad
Preparing our Hearts

Scripture: Mark 12:30; Deuteronomy 6:5-9

We worked in a difficult church where some key people showed disrespect and seemed to fight us at every turn. It was hard. I felt stifled and wished things would change. But one Sunday, as I was leading worship, God broke through my sadness and hurt, and I felt myself grasp what it means to love God with your heart, soul, mind, and strength — with our whole selves — as I let go and trusted God with abandon. It was like I put all the concerns and grief into his hands and released them, trusting him, praising him, and leaving all the details with him. That feeling of total freedom and trust in God is what I think he wants when he says for us to love him with all our hearts, souls, minds, and strength.

The commandment to obey is the most important commitment we make as believers. He says he is a jealous God, which some people misinterpret from a human understanding of jealousy. However, it means that he does not accept a half-hearted commitment. A half-hearted commitment is not a commitment. He wants all of us, if we are to be his followers.

But the bigger picture shows us that as we love him and honor him this way, he blesses us with freedom and joy. Nothing on this earth matches it. We can only find this kind of fruit from God. He gives us peace that surpasses our understanding when we love him as he deserves.

Prayer: If we ever find ourselves wrapped up in the world and circumstances around us, we can ask God to help us truly love him with our entire self and trust him with abandon. We can pray today that God shows us anywhere that we are holding back in our commitment to him and to help us love and trust him completely, with our whole lives and all we are.

Preparing to Parent

You may want to talk about how we love lots of things, but we mean different things when we say love. I love ice cream. I love my mom and dad. I love God. I love playing soccer. I love the weather. I love my new shoes. I love my best friend. I love my puppy. I love my teddy bear.

Do we mean the same thing when we say these?

How is one different from another?

We can discuss this, but most kids understand the difference naturally. However, we can help them have the words to describe what they are feeling. That is key. Many children do not have the words to truly express what they are thinking or feeling. So, we can give them those tools to help them help us to understand.

We can teach them the Greek words: agape (God's love, unconditional, commitment love), storge (familial love), philia (brotherly, friendship love), eros (passionate, sexual love), and philautos (self love). Or we can give them words like: delicious, favorite, fondness, friendship, commitment, important, closest, proud of, enjoy being with. We can teach them angry, frustrated, disappointed, sad, lonely, afraid, bored, and other words that share nuances of feeling.

Giving our children the language to express a variety of feelings is a great gift. Many picture books have been written that help with this, and one of those series is Diane Alber's Spot series of books. She clearly describes feelings where a child can understand. Another book about anger that is very good is *Angry Me* by Sandra V. Feder.

Then, we must help our children understand that real love, the kind of love God has for us and we have for him, is much more than a feeling. Feelings change with whatever happens. But real love, agape love, is a commitment to God and to a person. It loves even when we feel angry. This love has action where we try to meet the other person's needs, even when they are our enemies. God says when we meet other people's needs, it is like we are ministering to him. And he always loves us with Agape love, helping us, loving us, and staying with us always.

For the Family
Enjoying the Lesson Together

Scripture: Deuteronomy 6:5-9; Mark 12:30
    (remember to choose a verse as your family memory verse with each lesson)

Object Lesson: Person Puzzle

The Bible tells us to love the Lord with all our heart, soul, mind, and strength. It's kind of like this verse cuts our lives into four areas, but we can't be divided into four pieces and still be a whole person, can we? We're just one person. Let's look at our puzzle person.

When we put the heart section on the table, is he a whole person? If he loves God with all his heart, is he loving God with all he is? No. What if we add the soul? Is he loving God will his whole life? If we add the mind, is he whole? No, we must have all four parts to be a whole person. So, why do you think the Bible lists out all four areas?

If we love God with all our mind, that means we know about Jesus and about the Bible and all the things we should be doing, right? We would be very smart about how to love God. We would be careful about how we thought about people and things, trying to keep a good attitude maybe. We might think about how to defend what the Bible says and be able to talk to people about what the Bible tells us. But without our heart, we might just be arguing with people. We might know the right things to do but not choose to do what's right.

If we only love God with our heart, that means our emotions and feelings. We would think about how wonderful God is and get emotional maybe when we think about how amazing he is. We might plead with people that they need Jesus in their lives. We would love God with all our feelings, but we wouldn't have any real commitment. If we woke up feeling bad, we might be angry with God that day and not follow him at all. Our lives would be crazy like a roller coaster.

If we only love God with all our soul, we might be very religious but not build a real relationship with God. We would live a do/don't do rule-following life. We would do what the pastor told us to do without questioning or thinking about it. We would just do what we thought was right and would make us a good Christian, but the effort wouldn't go any deeper in our lives. We would be at church every time the doors were open. We give money to the church and make sure others see us being such a good person. But we wouldn't really know God and love him.

If we only loved God with our strength, we might go on mission trips, work to help the homeless, and do a lot of good things, trying to make God love us and people think we're good people, but we wouldn't know God and love him.

To be a real follower of Jesus, we must love him with our whole lives. Yes, we try to do the right things, know what the Bible says, and do good to others, but it all comes from loving God first. It's exciting to think about how loving God affects every part of our lives, and we love God with all of who we are.

Prayer/Song/Poem: Sing "Love the Lord Your God" by Lincoln Brewster.

Activity: Puzzle

Just for fun, work a puzzle together as a family or get small puzzles for each person to do.

Before you do this activity with your family, put the puzzle together yourself and turn it over. Write your memory verse on the back of the puzzle, and then, when your family puts it together, you can turn it over and practice your memory verse for the week.

If you do small puzzles, put each one together and write a note to each child and give them a verse to look up and share with the family. Once they complete their puzzle, they can turn over their puzzle and read the verse to the family. They can read the note aloud if they want, but they can also keep that for themselves if they prefer. We used to put a note of encouragement and what we saw God doing in that child's life.

Turning puzzles over: If it's a smaller puzzle, it's not a problem to turn it over. It usually stays together enough for someone to flip it over quickly. For the larger puzzles, you may need to work the puzzle on a board and put another board on top of it before you turn it over to hold it together. However, even if it falls apart a little, usually it is easy to reassemble once it's flipped over.

Picture Books: *Chasing God's Glory* by Dorina Lazo Gilmore-Young, *This I Know* by Clay Anderson, *Hear O Little One* by Eric Schrotenboer

heart mind

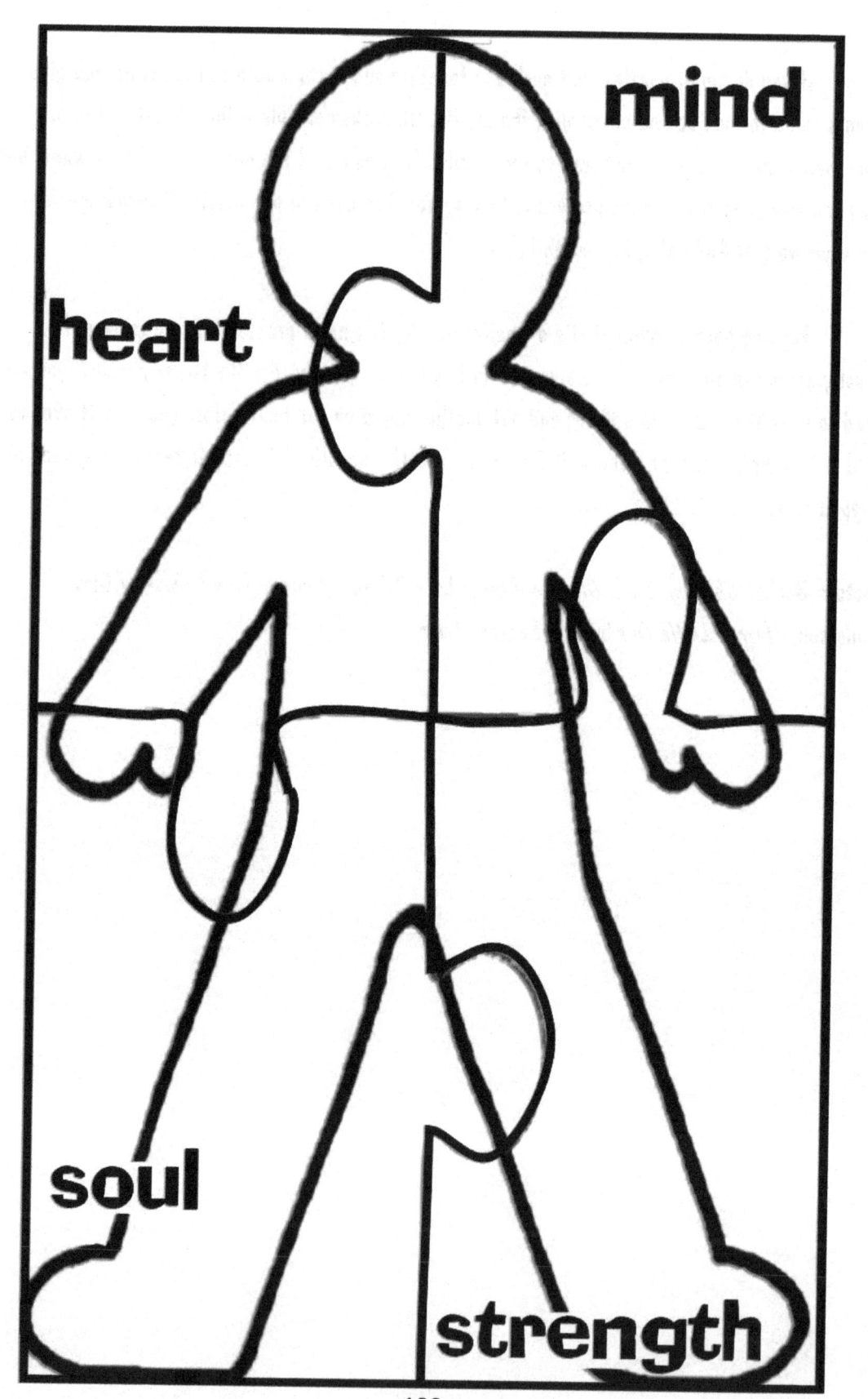

soul strength

Love (Others)

For Mom and Dad
Preparing our Hearts

Scripture: 1 John 4:7-21; 1 John 3:1; 1 Corinthians 13:1-13

We worked in a church that has around 13 countries represented on any given Sunday. Even though we were Baptist, most of those in our congregation had never even been to a Baptist church before. This created an interesting and wonderful atmosphere in our church, and we experienced amazing unity that we know was preserved by the Holy Spirit working in our midst. However, sometimes politics got in the way. One such time was when a young woman from South Africa came to our house to tell us how much she hated Americans. In fact, she said, we were the only Americans she liked. She admitted we were the only ones she had ever met. She spewed her hatred for our country, but we appreciated her coming to talk to us rather than to say things to others. My husband is an amazing man, if I do say so myself. That day, I left the room because I was very hurt by some of the things this woman was saying, and I didn't know how to process that anger quickly. With God's help, I remained great friends with this young woman, but at that moment, I needed to leave the room. Dave, however, continued the conversation with her for quite a while. He showed concern, empathy, and interest in all she had to share. She was hurting for the terrible things that had happened in her country and the many people who had been hurt. Most of her country blames the USA for their situation. I don't know all the ins and outs of all that happened there, but I do know that I learned a great deal about loving others that day.

1 John 4 is such a great scripture to remind us of God's expectation and requirement that we love him and others. It also reminds us that the love we have for others is not something

we muster ourselves. It comes from him. I'm so thankful for that because I would be terrible at loving others on my own.

Praise God that he loved us first, and he gave us the ability to love others. He fills us with his love and enables us to see others the way he sees them and the way he loves them. If we are having trouble loving someone, we must rely on God's power in us to help us break through our fear, hurt, anger, hesitation, or whatever is in the way.

Prayer: If we are ever having trouble loving or forgiving someone, we need to pray. God will help us. He will help us also remember all he has done for us, and we should extend that same grace to others.

Preparing to Parent

As our children get older, being sure they know what love really means is important. 1 Corinthians 13 is a beautiful description of true, agape love. The whole chapter calls us to a higher kind of love than we often see, it is a commitment type of love. It is love mixed with respect and integrity. In a culture that often equates love with selfishness and sexual interactions, helping our children understand real love can save them a great deal of heartache as they get older.

Verses 4-7 clearly describe a kind of love that puts the other person first and trusts the other person. Love is patient and kind. These words alone can help a young teen beginning to think of dating have higher expectations so that they recognize when they are being pushed into an unhealthy relationship.

For the Family
Enjoying the Lesson Together

Scripture: Matthew 25:31-46; 1 John 4:7-8; 1 John 3:1
(remember to choose a verse as your family memory verse with each lesson)

Object Lesson: Sharing God's Love with Others

Supplies needed:
Sponges (in the shapes of hearts are bonus)
Water
2 Small cups for each person
1 Large container

Fill the large container with water. That represents God's love. In reality, no container can hold all of God's love because his love never ends. But for now, we're going to use this showing that God has so much love for us and for the world.

Each person puts their sponge in the large container filling it with water, and squeezes out the water into a cup. When we fill up with God's love, we share it with others, and even when we feel we're running out of love, we go back to God, and he fills us up again. His love is never ending, and we can always be filled with his love for others if we go to him and his word.

Now, we're going to have a contest just for fun. Who can fill their two cups with water the fastest.

In real life, it's not a contest, but we do want to always remember that because God fills us with his love, we can always share love with others, and God commands us to do that.

Read the verses together.

Prayer/Song/Poem: A few songs are on YouTube about loving one another and the world knowing we are God's by our love. If you don't have time to look up one that you want to teach your children, you can use this simple one to the tune of "Are You Sleeping."

Love each other
Love each other
Love God too

God has lavished
God has lavished
His great love

Love God too
This way we show God's love
This way we show God's love
To the world
To the world

His great love
Making us his children
Making us his children
Now we love too
Now we love too

Activity: Word Search with Secret Message

Work the word search puzzle. It has a hidden message in the puzzle.

Picture Books: *Maybe I Can Love My Neighbor Too* by Jennifer Grant, *Will You Be Friends with Me?* by Kathleen Long Bostrom, *Somebody Loves You, Mr. Hatch* by Eileen Spinelli

```
W S E L O V O H B R O T H E R
E R B E M C D O C A N D Y C A
F E A U E O S M S E A H O R E
A G F A G I M E R U S Z T G T
M R N S F L O W E R S L Z O V
I U E D U S M A E R C E C I B
L B L T O Y S E V D O H J O P
Y M O G A G N I D A E R O R B
U A O H R P L K S D I K E E A
O H H F C A D T F T S F L H S
S O C C E R N N P S E F B C E
M U S I C N U D A A T R I A B
S E I N N U B H M R R A B E A
F R I E N D S X C A G K C T L
S E I L F R E T T U B N S K L
```

art	baseball	bible	books	brother
bunnies	butterflies	candy	cats	church
dad	dogs	family	flowers	friends
God	grandma	grandpa	hamburgers	home
ice cream	Jesus	mom	music	ocean
parks	pizza	reading	school	sister
soccer	teacher	toys		

___ ____ _____ ____ ____ _____ ____

_____ ___

This puzzle is a word search puzzle that has a hidden message in it. First find all the words in the list.
Words can go in any direction and share letters as well as cross over each other.
Once you find all the words. Copy the unused letters starting in the top left corner into the blanks to reveal the hidden message.

Look (at the flowers and birds)

For Mom and Dad
Preparing our Hearts

Scripture: Mathew 6:25-34

When we were missionaries, often money was scarce. We learned to trust God to provide, but as a mom, sometimes I battled my own fears and worry. I found a lily ring at a night market for less than $1, and I bought it. Any time I found myself worrying about food or money, I would wear that ring to remind me of these scriptures. It would cause me to pray and trust rather than worry. The other part of my worry was always trying to figure out what to do to try to solve the problem myself. I could take on another student in tutoring. I could ask my parents for money. Any number of desperate, terrible ideas that would cause more problems than solutions, and remembering these verses helped me to stop and wait, trust and pray.

When we read verses like Matthew 6, we know that God understands the human heart very well. He knows where we are going to struggle in our walk with him and what is going to trip us up in our faith. So, he prepares us. He tells us what to do and how we should approach life's challenges. We can be encouraged that God knows everything, and he has every situation in his capable hands. We just need to trust him and obey.

I encourage you, dear Mom or Dad, if you are concerned about how you're going to provide for your little ones, to embrace this lesson. Our God is a good God. He will provide for his people. He will meet our needs. We have seen it so many times in our lives and in the lives of our friends from having food not only for our family but enough to share, money for trips home miraculously provided, and even seeing fuel last in the gas tank of our car longer than it should have. God is trustworthy. When we take the time and actually look at the birds and flowers, another interesting effect happens. We relax as we look at them. We find peace just by watching nature in addition to being reminded of God's character and promises. Once we recognize God's sovereignty and experience his peace, we can hear him speaking much more clearly if he does want us to do something. Sometimes he will tell us to wait, rest, and trust, and sometimes he may put on our hearts to do something. However, if we are doing something, we are, hopefully, doing it at his prompting and not from our frantic worrying and seeking our own solutions. God has our lives in his hands, and he cares for each one of us. He will provide.

Prayer: We must pray. We must let go of our worry and fretting and trust God. We can bring our struggles and failures to God. Maybe we have put ourselves into this situation by over-spending. Maybe we are worried about our child's safety or future. We can bring all our concerns to him and trust him with everything on our hearts. He will help us. He still cares even though we aren't perfect. We should spend time praying for all these concerns today.

Preparing to Parent

As parents, we try to protect our children. We shouldn't be sharing every adult worry and concern with them. They are not equipped to emotionally handle it all. However, sometimes, we may want to have them share in the prayers, especially if the whole family is praying about a big purchase such as a car or house. Having our children join in can be powerful in their lives.

We may hesitate because we fear God won't provide a way for us to buy that car or house. This is where we need to use wisdom and discernment. Is God leading us to buy a new car because we now have four children who don't fit in our little economy car? Or do we just think we should buy a new car because we're tired of our old one? If we know we have a need, not just a want, we can involve our children in praying. We always admit that God is in control, and in his timing, he will answer our prayers, but we trust him through it all, especially in the waiting.

Our children learn great lessons about faith and prayer when we involve them in these times. The more we worry and strive to solve problems in our strength, our children also learn that. Granted, we are not perfect. We are going to fail at times and give in to worry, but we can help our children learn faith instead if we are careful, honest, and truly seek to obey God's word in our walk.

For the Family
Enjoying the Lesson Together

Scripture: Mathew 6:25-30
    (remember to choose a verse as your family memory verse with each lesson)

Object Lesson: Observing Nature: Birds and Flowers

Ideally, we want to go out in nature and observe the birds and flowers. If it is winter, we can put a pinecone covered in peanut butter and bird seed out for the winter birds and watch them enjoy our gift. We can look at pictures of flowers or spend time looking at a Christmas cactus or poinsettia.

However, if we are in spring or summer, we can enjoy God's beautiful creation all around us. We can take a family trip to a local park, botanical garden, or bird sanctuary, but we can probably enjoy God's provision in our own backyard.

After spending some time observing and commenting on the colors and beauty, we can go to our patio or dinner table and let the children draw some flowers and birds while we read the scriptures together. They can then write their memory verse on their picture and put it up on the wall or fridge to help with memorizing.

    Ask if they ever worry about anything. Let them share.
    Why does the Bible tell us not to worry?
    What does God promise in these verses?
    Can we trust God? Will he provide for our needs?
    What should we do if we start worrying?

Prayer/Song/Poem: Pray together about the things that tempt each of you to worry, and if you are praying for God's provision for a big item, pray about that together too. Encourage each child to pray at least a sentence prayer aloud.

Activity: Give away clothes, food, and toys.

One reason this activity can be so powerful is that we tend to hang on to things for fear we won't have something when we need it, or we value things too much. Giving things away helps us to let go of the hold things have on us and helps us trust God to provide what we need when we need it.

Picture Books: *Those Shoes* by Maribeth Boelts, *Lord, I Worry* by Aaron Hoover, *Wemberly Worried* by Kevin Henkes

Tell (the truth)

For Mom and Dad
Preparing our Hearts

Scripture: Zechariah 8:16-17; Proverbs 14:25; Proverbs 12:22-23; Jeremiah 17:9-10; John 8:31-32

My mother was a strong woman of God, but one thing she taught me to do well was lie. I know that seems completely weird to say, but she was really good at putting a spin on things. For instance, if I didn't feel great, and we wanted to take a personal day (those didn't exist when I was a kid), she would call the school and tell them I wasn't feeling well and needed to stay home. Technically, it was the truth, but it was really a lie. I wasn't sick. I wanted to stay home.

It is hard to be completely honest sometimes. We can easily put a spin on our situation or rationalize our lies for whatever "good" reason we come up with. We also are tempted to lie to save face, to make ourselves look better, or to try not to hurt someone. We even lie to ourselves without even realizing it until God opens our eyes.

God calls us to be honest and to do what is right. How can we have any hope of truly being honest trustworthy people?

1. We listen to the Holy Spirit when he pricks our conscience, repent, and make it right.
2. We learn and know God's word. It is truth, and it will help us hold on to truth.
3. We pray for God to reveal lies we're believing and sharing.

4. We ask God to renew our minds and help us be honest with ourselves and others.
5. We determine to tell the truth even when it is uncomfortable.

Prayer: Pray for God to protect us from the enemy and his lies. Ask him to help us be honest and trustworthy. Ask God to renew our minds.

Preparing to Parent

As parents, we must be honest with our children. That doesn't mean we tell them everything, of course. They don't need to know everything going on, especially things that could cause them to worry. However, whatever they ask about, we must be honest with them with an age-appropriate response. If they ask something that seems too heavy or advanced for their ages, a simple answer that satisfies their question is appropriate. The reason for this is simple. We want them to know they can always come to us with their questions, and we will give them a straight answer. We will not lie to them. We are trustworthy.

This is why I never told my kids that Santa Claus and the Tooth Fairy were real. We still played with the ideas at times, and they still got money when they lost a tooth and "Santa" presents under the tree for fun, but they knew the truth. Our focus at Christmas has always been Christ, worship at church, and doing service or sharing the Gospel.

Another area parents sometimes struggle with telling the truth is when our kids get older and ask embarrassing questions like, "Did you ever smoke pot?" or whatever sinful, rebellious thing we might have done. We chose to be honest with our kids in every instance. It wasn't a big deal in the long run. Perhaps we are afraid that sharing our own rebellion somehow makes it seem to our children that we are giving them permission to rebel as well. But we found we were able to share with them the consequences of our actions and the regret we felt, and it encouraged them to make better choices. Honesty needs to go beyond sharing what we did in rebellion to God to the full testimony of what we learned, how God saved us and forgave us, and what consequences we still faced because of any sinful choices we made.

We can't control their choices, and they will make their own decisions. If they choose to rebel as well, we've given them the information they need to find their way back. We want them to know that God still loves them and will forgive them. How terrible it would be to not be honest and cause our children to feel they can never find their way back because we've painted a false picture of the Christian life. We aren't perfect, and they aren't perfect, but our God's mercy and grace is. He is the only one who expresses love perfectly, and he will always welcome home the prodigal.

For the Family
Enjoying the Lesson Together

Scripture: Proverbs 12:22-23; Proverbs 14:25
   (remember to choose a verse as your family memory verse with each lesson)

Object Lesson: 2 Truths and a Lie — Animal Edition

First, teach your children to hold both hands up high if they think the fact is a truth and to make their arms create an X if they think the "fact" is a lie. (Note: In each set of three sentences below, the bolded item is the lie.)

1. **Mommy opossums hang by their tails**
2. An African dog called the Basenji doesn't bark like other dogs
3. Cats can make over 100 vocal sounds

1. Dalmatians are born without spots
2. Hummingbirds are the only birds that can fly backwards
3. **Touching a toad will give you warts**

1. Crocodiles cannot stick out their tongues
2. The only flying mammal is a bat
3. **Bats are blind**

1. Butterflies taste with their feet
2. **Bulls become angry when they see red**
3. Polar Bears have black skin

1. Sloths only poop once a week
2. Kangaroos cannot pass gas
3. **Camels store water in their humps**

1. **Bears hibernate**
2. Rats laugh when tickled
3. Only female mosquitoes bite

1. Slugs have four noses
2. Octopuses have three hearts
3. **Goldfish have a three-second memory span**

1. **Ostriches bury their heads in the sand**
2. Reindeer eyeballs turn blue in the winter
3. Squirrels cannot burp

1. **Koalas are bears**
2. Honeybees can flap their wings 200 times every second
3. Horses use facial expressions to communicate with each other

1. Giraffes communicate with their eyebrows during the day
2. Seagulls can drink saltwater
3. **Sharks float easily in saltwater**

The best way to finish this object lesson would be to read Elizabeth Urbanowicz book *What Is Truth?* However, if you don't have that available, talk about how we can be fooled by lies, and we can fool others by lies. While the game is fun, in real life, how would you feel if someone tried to get you to believe a lie? How would you feel if someone told a lie about you to other people?

Read verses

Why do you think God wants us to tell the truth? How can we remind ourselves to tell the truth?
Prayer/Song/Poem: Pray for God to help you tell the truth and know the truth.

Activity: That's a Good Question

If you have some conversation starter cards, this is a great time to do some of those encouraging each person to be totally honest because we are always safe in our family to share the truth. If you don't have conversation starter cards, think of some questions you'd like to explore with your children. They can be as simple as what their dreams are for their future; what they hope to accomplish during this school year; who their best friend is and why.

Let them ask you questions too.

Picture Books: *What Is Truth?* by Elizabeth Urbanowicz, *Chameleon's Can of Worms* by J. D. Camorlina, *Arlo and the Great Big Cover-Up* by Betsy Childs, *Finn's Little Fibs* by Tom Percival

Keep (what is good)

For Mom and Dad
Preparing our Hearts

Scripture: 1 Thessalonians 5:16-24; 2 Corinthians 10:5; Philippians 4:8

When I was younger, I struggled with depression. My friend, who also battles it, one day said, "This can't be God's plan for our lives." Her words struck my heart, and I felt the same way. I knew my depression was mild compared to some. I was not on medication. However, I struggled. I prayed and did some research. I began to recognize that one little event or comment would start me spiraling down into depression, and I found during those times I focused on thoughts that did not glorify God. I began focusing on the truth, and stopped filling my mind with "news," and re-examined comments and events that sent me down the rabbit hole of emotions.

When I was in journalism as a student, our teachers drilled into us that no one should be able to tell what our opinion is when they read our articles. We were only to report the story. That notion has changed in our culture today, and much of what we see on the news is sensationalized and politicized. It is causing depression and hopelessness for many people. I made a conscious decision to stop watching the news and limited my social media interactions. Sometimes we need to consider making choices like this to honor God and to protect our minds.

We need to apply Philippians 4:8 daily to our lives, taking every thought captive and asking God to renew our minds. This way we can find victory over this kind of self-inflicted depression. We can, instead, focus on ministering to others and putting others before ourselves. We can put away what is not beneficial and keep what is good.

Prayer: When we struggle with depression or self-defeating thoughts, we can ask God to renew our minds and to help us seize every thought. We can pray for God to help us find ways to hold onto what is good and to get rid of what is not. We can honor God with our thoughts and attitudes if we learn to obey these verses.

Preparing to Parent

We've talked often about helping our children recognize lies about God and the world and accepting the truth. We encourage critical thinking. However, when it comes to believing lies about ourselves, it can be more difficult. As parents, it's much harder to combat this behavior in our children if we fall into the "building self-esteem" trap. This trap can lead to a more self-focused narcissistic lifestyle in our children rather than achieving the desired goal of helping them become independent and confident. Or, we may wish to alleviate their pain through medication. (Granted, people have different views about medication. I fall on the side of less medication is best for myself and my family. You must pray, as the parent, and discern what is best for your child. However, if you are treating depression alone, I firmly urge you to work with your medical team to find the root cause first and try to deal with it in other ways when possible.). We don't want to fail our children by not helping them understand that what they think about affects their emotions. The medication may not help if they think about negative things and focus on lies about themselves.

This is a tough issue, and I don't pretend to have all the answers. However, I do encourage parents to seriously pray for wisdom and guidance. God knows what our children need and how we can help them. We can trust him. If our children do need medication, we need to have peace about that choice and not allow what others think to discourage us.

And, whatever other measures we might take to help our children, we need to help them learn how to control their thought life and take negative thoughts captive. They too must learn to live out the Philippians verse. We can help them limit the damaging influences from news, social media, gaming, and television. If we can keep conversations open with our children at any age, we will find it helps us and them to keep on top of these influences and thought life.

We must speak truth and help our children remember that Satan is the father of lies, and he seeks to destroy God's plan in our lives. One of the best ways he can do that is by getting us distracted with negative thoughts or worse. He will try to convince us and our children that God cannot use our lives, that we are useless, and our lives are worthless. He is evil. That's not an adjective as much as it's a noun when talking about Satan. But God is good. And greater is he who is in us than he who is in the world. We can help our children find victory. In prayer and conversation with them, we can fight for their mental and spiritual health. We are in a battle, but we can do this, and we can win with God's help and guidance.

For the Family
Enjoying the Lesson Together

Scripture: 1 Thessalonians 5:16-18, 21-22, Philippians 4:8
(remember to choose a verse as your family memory verse with each lesson)

Object Lesson: Sorting

Ideally, this lesson is best with sorting grapes, grape tomatoes, or blackberries looking for the good ones and throwing out the bad ones. However, to make it simpler, you can use skittles, m&m's, beads, counting bears, or other small items that can be sorted by color.

If using colored items, you have to choose one color that is the "bad" color for today. We want to sort out the bad and keep the good.

After sorting, while children enjoy the fruit of their labor if you've used edible items, read the verses. Ask what are some things we need to sort out as bad? They may need you to give them some ideas since this is a little harder, such as if someone gossips or says something mean about someone else. If someone calls us a mean name. If we have mean thoughts. If we sin and think we shouldn't talk to God about it. If we think we are a terrible person God doesn't love. Thoughts and words that are not true need to be thrown away.

What are some things we should keep? Bible verses. True statements. Good thoughts. Kindness. Being Thankful.

How does that help us? When we believe the truth and throw away lies, we are happier and more peaceful.

Prayer/Song/Poem: Read

Activity: Scripture copying.

This is always a good activity with any lesson you are doing that includes scripture. These verses are such important reminders of how we are to live as disciples, they seem like a good choice to focus on copying.

For the youngest children, find the page they can trace and copy it for them. For your older children, they can copy the verses themselves.

Picture Books: *God Made Me in His Image* by Justin S. Holcomb and Lindsey A. Holcomb, *Bad Seed* by Jory John, *Being Frank* by Donna W. Earnhardt

Never give up.

A boy of joy.

Always be yourself.

Whatever you do, keep praying.

Happy thinking.

His now is your.

We in Christ Jesus.

He was tempted.

Ephesians 6:18-19.

Share

For Mom and Dad
Preparing our Hearts

Scripture: Romans 12:13; 1 Thessalonians 2:8; 2 Timothy 2:2; Hebrews 13:16; 1 Peter 4:9; Proverbs 22:9; Acts 2:42-47; Romans 12:9-13; 2 Corinthians 9:12-15

We were coming out of the restaurant, and my daughter had quite a bit of her food left in a take-out box. By the parking lot sat a young man, obviously homeless. My daughter asked if she could give him her leftover food. I didn't know how he would respond or if he'd be okay eating her leftovers, but we told her she could try. He was very grateful, and she was happy she could bless him.

Sometimes we may feel a little hesitant or concerned to let our children share with homeless people or others in need, but when it is safe, it can be a life-changing experience. Putting feet to their faith makes their faith stronger, the same as it does our own.

We are called to share our faith, share our belongings, and share our homes. We should never underestimate the power of sharing, especially sharing hospitality. Through hospitality, people are connected in community. These simple acts of sharing bring healing and wholeness to the body of Christ and often lead people to open their hearts to the Gospel. Fellowship and hospitality are two of the most powerful ways we can share God's love especially in our world that is more connected to electronics than to people.

Preparing to Parent

One important fact we need to clarify often for our children, especially when they are heading into Middle School age, is that Communism/Socialism and what Jesus talked about are two very different things. For some reason, at that age, the simplistic view of those three beliefs seems to be congruent in their understanding. It's not true sharing as God tells us to do if we're forced through the government systems of Communism and Socialism to give up what we have so others can have it.

Jesus calls us to share through generosity and hospitality. We still have this same calling even when times are difficult, but the calling is much less effective when governments take all or nearly all people have.

Explaining the differences becomes a vital part of protecting our young people from becoming angry and defensive about these ideas. The source of the confusion over, and the lies of Communism and Socialism is the Father of Lies and the Father of Confusion, Satan. He wants to cause division and confusion wherever he can, and he rejoices in the anger that separates families.

Therefore, we need to be sure our children understand the truth, and we need to be the first ones to teach them the truth, so they know to come to us when they are confused by what they are learning. It's much easier to teach truth than to clean up misguided confusion once it has been adopted as truth.

Today, more than ever, we are seeing the necessity for this.

For the Family
Enjoying the Lesson Together

Scripture: Romans 12:13; 1 Thessalonians 2:8; 2 Timothy 2:2; Hebrews 13:16; 1 Peter 4:9; Proverbs 22:9; Romans 12:9-13
(remember to choose a verse as your family memory verse with each lesson)

Object Lesson: Jumping in Puddles

If you don't have a rainy day for this activity, you can play in the sprinkler in your yard. Usually, a puddle can be created as the children play. Or they can splash in a small pool and have the same results.

The objective is to splash as much water on everyone as possible. Use super soakers or whatever you have for a fun day in the water or jump whole-heartedly into puddles and splash each other mercilessly. Everyone should have a fun time with lots of giggles.

After the water/puddle fun, sit down in the park or the backyard and talk about sharing. Sharing God's love is like splashing his love all around.

Ask: What kinds of things can we share to splash God's love around?
Keep a list of ideas because you may want to do them later as a family outing or project.

We share God's word and what he's done in our lives with others.
We share our homes and the things God's blessed us with.
When we see a need, sometimes God is telling us to share and meet that need.

Prayer/Song/Poem: Pray for God to open our eyes to see people who need God's love or have other needs we can meet.

Activity: Sharing Food with the Poor

Share food with the poor either by giving a meal to a homeless person or helping at a soup kitchen. Each child could clean out their toy box or closet and find items to donate to the poor.

Picture Books: *If Jesus Came to My House* by Joan G. Thomas, *Puddle* by Hyewon Yum, *Come On, Rain* by Karen Hesse, *Seeds for Sharing* by Carissa Lovvorn; *The Oil Lamp* by Dawn Stephens

Plant

For Mom and Dad
Preparing our Hearts

Scripture: Galatians 6:6-8; John 15:4

One of the most amazing times in my life was during my early high school years. I had come to a place in my Christian Walk where I wanted to be bold for Christ and not worry about what others thought. I began sharing my faith boldly with my friends. The majority of my friends at school were not believers. I shared sometimes in awkward ways and sometimes in terrible ways, but I shared from a heart that longed to see my friends know Christ. And God brought the harvest. It was wonderful. When I graduated from high school, I looked back, and nearly every friend had come to Christ. Now, many years later, I've reconnected with some on social media, and many are serving God, and their kids are going into missions and ministry or are actively serving God is other ways. God is so good, and he has brought a bountiful harvest that is still going. I'm so thankful I got to be a small part in it.

We reap what we sow in this life. We bear fruit because of what God is doing in and through us. However, we need to be intentional and obedient. We can't worry about what others think or how they will react. We just have to be faithful to share our stories of how Christ has changed our lives. Sometimes we may be awkward, and sometimes we may feel like we've done a terrible job of sharing, but we are planting seeds that God can grow.

If we are struggling to share our faith, we need to examine our hearts and see if fear is holding us back or if we are unsure of what we believe. Are we making excuses or rationalizing why we don't share? If we are sharing, even if we aren't seeing fruit, we need to understand a couple important points:

God brings the fruit, we don't. We are called to share and leave the results to God.

Fruit is more than seeing people come to Christ. Sometimes fruit is a change in our hearts or simply planting a seed of faith and God's love. If we are following Christ, we are bearing fruit even if we don't yet recognize it.

Prayer: Pray for boldness. We need it as we walk through a post-Christian world. People still need the Lord, and we still need to share. Pray that we will be obedient, bold, loving, and kind.

Preparing to Parent

As we read Mark 4 about the sower and the seeds, we recognize that not everyone we share our faith with is ready to hear it and embrace following Christ. Helping our children understand that will help them as they share. You can learn the 3 Circles of sharing faith, they teach about green, yellow, and red lights. We can teach this to our children as a simple way to understand when someone is not open to hearing the Gospel, and they'll be equipped to handle the situation well by offering to answer questions if ever the person they shared with wants to know more.

We also need to evaluate where our children's hearts are. Are they ready for the Gospel? Are they open or rebellious? Do they need more time? As parents, sometimes, we want to push. We want our children to choose Christ, and we can push them away if we are not careful.

We need to be patient and trust God. Yes, we need to share every time we can, but our expectations will determine how hard we push for them to make a decision. We need to drop the expectations and replace them with trust in God, the one who loves our children much more than we do and who wants them to come to him even more than we do. We need to share through our actions and words but recognize that our children may take time to choose Christ, and we can't play like we're the Holy Spirit. If we push too hard, we can push them away from God. We certainly don't want to do that.

For the Family

Enjoying the Lesson Together

Scripture: 1 Corinthians 5:6-8

    (remember to choose a verse as your family memory verse with each lesson)

Object Lesson: Planting Seeds

    Supplies Needed:
    Disposable cups
    Seeds
    Soil
    Water

This is a simple object lesson of planting seeds and watering them. The actual results will be seen over the next several weeks as God helps the seeds to grow.

As children plant the seeds, each child plants seeds in their own cup, and then they water another child's cup and let someone else water their cup.

We each have our part in making these plants, but it is God who makes them grow.

Then read the scriptures and talk about the metaphor of the Gospel being the seed we plant and water. How do we plant that seed? How do we water that seed? When someone decides to give their lives to Jesus and follow him, that is when we see the harvest that God brings.

Give each child a seed to keep reminding them they have the wonderful seed of the Gospel to share with the world.

Prayer/Song/Poem: Mary Rice Hopkins has a great song called "Sowing Seeds of Love" that fits well with this lesson.

Activity: Write your testimony

This activity is for your older children. For your younger children, you may want to have them read books or color while the older children work on writing out their testimonies.

Each believing child who is in 2nd grade or higher can do this activity to some degree.

1. For children the first part is optional: What my life was like before Jesus
2. How I knew I needed a Savior
3. How I became a Christian
4. My life since I've started following Christ
5. How I'm growing in my faith

If your children are willing, it would be wonderful to have them share their testimonies with the family. They should practice sharing it so they can share their faith in 1-3 minutes.

Picture Books: *Oh, the Seeds You Can Sow* by Jessica Lisk, *It Will Be Okay* by Lysa TerKeurst, *The Oak Inside the Acorn* by Max Lucado, *Wherever You Go, I Want You to Know* by Melissa B. Kruger

Listen

For Mom and Dad
Preparing Our Hearts

Scripture: Proverbs 1 and 4; Proverbs 8:1; James 1:5, 22; Psalm 46:10

One of my first years teaching, we were going through Genesis. I taught my lesson, then I had seminary class that evening. On the way home from seminary, something happened that I've never experienced before. As Dave drove us home from class, suddenly I found myself in God's presence like never before. It was not a happy experience, but one where he confronted me. He pointed out that I had compromised his word to try to make it fit with evolution. I was not sure if I was going to survive this encounter. I repented immediately and apologized to my students the next day telling them I had said some wrong things. We went back to the Bible, and I shared about the six days of Creation. After that, I began to do research into the science and theories surrounding Creationism and Evolution. I have taken my responsibility as a teacher much more seriously since that night, and I've sought to never compromise the Word of God. When we listen to the so-called wisdom of men and try to compromise the wisdom and truth of God, we are simply listening to the lies of the enemy.

We need godly wisdom and understanding. Without listening to God's word and the leading of the Holy Spirit, we walk in our own wisdom and understanding, but we need God's wisdom and guidance. We live in a world that does not seem to seek wisdom at all sometimes. Emotional reactions, staunch opinions, and loud rhetoric seem to rule the day.

We absolutely cannot compromise the Truth of God's Word to appease the world, to limit our fears, or to fit into our culture. God's Truth is real, and it's eternal. It never changes.

Psalm 46:10 reminds us to be still and know that he is God. In the context and original language of the verse, "be still" means relax, let go, stop striving, stop fighting. It fits well with what we need in our world today. Whether we're concerned about the opinions voiced through media or just striving to make ends meet, relaxing in God's presence can renew us and help us hear his voice in his word. We truly need these times of refreshing daily in God's presence, learning from him and his wisdom to guide us in our daily life.

Prayer: Life is challenging, and God wants us to bring our concerns to him. He welcomes us to pray for calmness, steadiness, and godliness throughout our days. We can pray for God to give us his wisdom daily and that we will listen to his word, hiding it in our hearts.

Preparing to Parent

The scriptures tell us to seek wisdom and understanding. As parents, there is not greater time that we need God's guidance and wisdom than when we are trying to guide our children and help them become the human beings God means for them to be? In fact, knowing that we can ask for and rely on God's wisdom, understanding, and mercy is what keeps us going as parents sometimes. How can we even hope to be successful without these?

James 1:22 reminds us that we can't just read God's word and listen to what it says, but we must apply God's word and act on it. Listening is imperative, but acting brings that listening into practice.

How do we listen? As parents we need to listen to our children to understand what they are going through, what their needs are, what understanding or misunderstanding they are gaining, and what they are asking of us. Then, we need to listen to God as he guides us in our own walk with him and in parenting our children. He will give us insight into their needs and the wisdom to know how to best help them navigate all they are going through as they grow. Finally, we take what God teaches us, and we teach it to our children. We help them seek wisdom and understanding in their lives, and then we must also help them apply what they've learned and live it.

Listening is vital, but application is too.

For the Family
Enjoying the Lesson Together

Scripture: Proverbs 1 and 4; Proverbs 8:1
(remember to choose a verse as your family memory verse with each lesson)

Object Lesson: Listening to each other and listening to stories.

In this object lesson, we will practice listening.

Give each person a notebook (if your children don't write yet, they can draw what they hear.)

You may choose to use conversation starter cards such as the ones available on my website: terriehellardbrown.com/product/spark-a-conversation-cards/ or simply have each person say something about how they feel or what they are thinking about. You could ask each person to answer the question: What was the most interesting thing that happened in our day today?

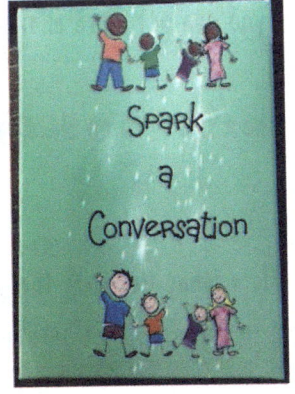

Each person takes a turn answering. After they answer, the person on their left will say what they heard. The first person will say "yes, that's right" or "no" and explain again.

Repeat this until the first person feels heard. Usually, the child or person sharing will smile and feel so affirmed that they were heard correctly. It's a simple exercise, but it is powerful. It really is a wonderful tool to use when someone has a disagreement or feels misunderstood.

A second part of the lesson is to tell or read a story, then have your child retell the story. Talk about listening and how important it is to listen to others and especially to listen to God. Share a favorite Bible story and ask each child to retell it and then tell what they learned about God or about something we should do or not do in the story.

Prayer/Song/Poem: Pray for God to help each of us listen to his word and obey it. Pray for each of us to grow in wisdom and understanding. And then pray that we can each listen to one another.

Activity: The Flip Flop Obstacle Course

This is a fun game to play if your kids are in for a crazy good time.
Supplies:
Squishy toys, stuffed animals, or other toys that won't hurt if you step on them
Flippers for swimming
Sleeping mask

Set up a path or obstacle course created with soft toys. Depending on the age of your children, you can put more challenging obstacles in their path.

The child puts on the flippers and mask. Help them stand at the starting point of the course.

Then, they listen to the person's voice who is helping them navigate the obstacle course. Tell them to focus on that person's voice and obey it.

All the other family members stand around the course saying the wrong ways to go. The child walking through the course must concentrate on the right voice and act accordingly.

Let each child try to walk through the course this way.

When they get to the end of the course, point out three important lessons:

We must listen to the right voice (God's voice/God's word, our parents' voices) to know the truth, to gain wisdom, and to know what to do.

When we hear God's voice through his word, we must obey. If we hear our parents telling us to do something, we must obey. If we don't obey, it is like we weren't really listening.

Sometimes it isn't easy to obey, but just because it is hard doesn't mean we don't do it. Walking in flippers is not easy, but you did it anyway! That's awesome.

Another activity is to paint story stones and practice retelling stories. You can find the class for how to make them on my YouTube channel: https://youtu.be/AdDU741bSQk You can only access it with the link.

Picture Books: *Grumpy Monkey* by Suzanne Lang, *Yes I Can Listen* by Steve Metzger, *Howard Wigglebottom Learns to Listen* by Reverend Ana and Howard Binkow

How I Hear Him by Rachael Macaluso: I listed this book separately for two reasons: it is the only children's Christian book I found about listening to God, and it has one illustration I take issue with where it shows a girl doing yoga. One of the pages has an explanation that I think some may misunderstand, but overall, this is done very well. I would just discuss the problem with the picture and make sure my child understands the truth and is not assuming incorrect ideas. This is a hard concept for many believers, but this book handles it very well.

Look (at the ants)

For Mom and Dad
Preparing our Hearts

Scripture: Proverbs 6:6-11, Genesis 1-3, Leviticus 23:3, Romans 12:8-12

When my best friend and I were on a mission trip (he later became my husband), we spent time in a park where we'd been witnessing and handing out gospel tracts. As we took a short break on a park bench, we watched some ants. Soon, we were making up conversations between the ants and a whole little play was happening before us. It was silly and fun, but one thing was obvious – those ants were busy!

I'm so thankful that God calls us to have a Sabbath each week, but that is because we are expected to work hard. Sometimes we think that work is a part of the fall, that we have to work because of sin. Actually, Genesis tells us we'll have to work harder to make things grow well in the garden because of sin, but Adam worked in the garden long before sin entered the picture; it was just much easier. Work is a gift from God. It gives us a sense of purpose and accomplishment. We should be grateful for the work of our hands and honor God with it.

We need to set a good example for our children and work hard while still honoring God with our rest and keeping our family as a priority. It can be a difficult balancing act, but we must try to keep our lives in order and balanced, but we can never be lazy. Even on a day off that is not our Sabbath, if we want to gain wealth and keep our home in shape, we should work and never be lazy.

Whether we are keeping the Sabbath or working hard, we can bring our children along with us on some of our activities. By keeping our relationships with our family and with God at the center of our lives we show our children what it is like to worship God and rest in him.

Prayer: We should pray that we can balance our work and rest. We can pray that we are good examples for our children to follow. We can pray for God to show us where we are becoming too caught up in our work or where we are being lazy.

Preparing to Parent

One of the best things we can do as parents is to allow our children to work alongside us. We can let them help cook a meal, fix something in the garage, or work in the garden. Helping them understand the value of work is important as they grow into adulthood.

Another way we can help them learn to appreciate work is in play. We let them play house, but we can include items to allow for playing "work" as well. We can include order form tablets, paper products, a calculator (with a paper roll is even more fun), a toy cash register and toy store, empty boxes from food items, a briefcase, a typewriter. Playing vet, hospital, school, and other types of work play helps too. In this way they are trying on different careers, and they are learning that adults work to provide for their families and to bless their communities.

What are some ways we can include our kids this week in our work?

For the Family
Enjoying the Lesson Together

Scripture: Proverbs 6:6-11, Romans 12:11
(remember to choose a verse as your family memory verse with each lesson)

Object Lesson: Watch Ants

This is simple from the verses we're reading. We can literally look at ants and see how busy they are and how much they work.

Give each child a cookie or cracker and have them put some small crumbs down near the ants and watch what they do.

Encourage the children to talk about what they see and what they are learning from the ants. They can see hard work, cooperation, communication, strength, and community in watching the ants.

Then read the verses and talk about what God wants us to do and what kind of work they can help with around the house.

Prayer/Song/Poem: Sing "I'm Gonna Work" by Sing Hosanna

Pray about daily schedules and allow children to confess if they've been lazy or to commit their time to God each day and to work hard. Families can find all kinds of chore lists and schedule charts online that work well with children.

Activity: The Lazy Lose

Play a game where one person pretends to sleep surrounded by several items like toys, stuffed animals, or blocks, while everyone tries to sneak up and take things from around the person. If they hear the thieves and "wake up" they chase the person and tag them. Then they get the item back.

Take turns and see who catches the most thieves. Then talk about how being lazy doesn't add anything but allows things to be stolen. However, when we work hard, God blesses us and is pleased with us.

Picture Books: *The Gritty Little Lamb* by Dan Allbaugh, *Are You Working Hard or Hardly Working* by Bryan Smith, *A Different Pond* by Bao Phi, *Aesop's Fables the Ant and the Grasshopper* by Kelly Miles

Train

For Mom and Dad
Preparing our Hearts

Scripture: Proverbs 22:6; Ephesians 6:4

We'd resisted for years, but we finally accepted that we needed to get a dog. That may seem strange, but it was actually the result of us following the guidance of Proverbs 22:6. The original meaning of this verse is not just about teaching our children about the Lord like Deuteronomy 6 is. It is about helping our children follow the bent of their gifting, talents, and personalities. Our oldest daughter loves animals. And she has high-functioning autism. We realized a dog was an answer to her moving further into who God created her to be. It was amazing to witness the change in her. She accepted responsibility much better, became more relaxed overall, and has even become more social because of all that has happened since we got her a dog.

Proverbs 22:6 is not a promise but a guideline. The verse doesn't promise us that if we raise our children in the Lord, they will always follow him. There is no real formula for *making* someone follow Christ. We can teach faithfully, but we all still have free will, and God does not cross that line. We pray, and he draws people, but each person has the choice to make of whether to follow Christ or not. Our children also have free choice. So, what do we do? We do our best to teach them God's word and his ways. We help them fall in love with the God who loves them. And we trust God to keep them and lead them.

The Proverbs verse is about us helping our children find their way in the world so they can be who God intended them to be. They will follow in that, find that way, if we help lead them and teach them. It is a beautiful thing to see someone living in the gifts and calling God has given them.

Prayer: We need to pray that God will help us teach our children well and that we will have wisdom and discernment to see how God has gifted our children, so we can help lead them in that way.

Preparing to Parent

The second verse above is similar to the Great Commission and to Deuteronomy 6 that tells us to teach our children what we have learned from God. We need to take this command seriously, it is especially important today, living in a culture of deconstruction. But as we share what we have learned, we need to be aware if we are frustrating or overwhelming our children. We need to pray for our children and check their understanding of our teaching along the way.

In addition, we must pray about how we can help our children do ministry. We can encourage them to help in church. Maybe, if you are working in the nursery, your children can read books to the littler children, for example. If they can begin serving, they will be able to take ownership of their faith more easily.

Our teaching and leadership for our children is, therefore, twofold. We are to lead them in the way God created them to be, and we are to teach them all that God has taught us about following him.

For the Family
Enjoying the Lesson Together

Scripture: 1 Corinthians 9:24-27
    (remember to choose a verse as your family memory verse with each lesson)

Object Lesson: Obstacle Course

This can be as elaborate or as simple as you want. I've seen some courses created by families that rival the Gladiator courses on those TV shows. Or you can make one with sidewalk chalk and a jump rope or two. Whatever you decide, the idea is to help everyone do some athletic training.

If your children aren't athletic, you can opt for another kind of training such as a musical instrument, creating artwork, learning sign language or another language (we'll use this in the extra activity today), or even playing a game like Jenga and learning to improve a skill they have.

Then talk about the scriptures and how no one is good at what they are doing the first time they try it. They may have fun and do their best, but each person who is training to master something needs lots of practice. Training by practicing is how we get better and better at doing something. We must be patient and consistent in our training, or we won't progress.

As Christians we experience a similar thing. When we first choose to follow Jesus, we love him and thank him for saving us and for forgiving us, but we have a lot to learn in how to walk with him. We need to learn what the Bible says, and we need to learn how to pray, worship, and tell others about him. Everything we've been learning as a family has been for training in our Christian Walk. As we train, we get stronger in our faith and know God more and trust him more.

Prayer/Song/Poem: Signing a Song

Let's do some more training. We're going to learn some sign language as we learn to sing this song.

If you know some sign language, I recommend "Here I Am to Worship" from Rock Church and Sign Language Worship on YouTube. If sign language is completely new to you, then I recommend "Jesus Loves Me." Several videos show how to sign this song. You can also find several videos on YouTube of "Amazing Grace."

Activity: Signing Songs

YouTube has some great videos for kids and families that teach sign language words for church and school. As a family, you can learn these and be able to talk with someone who is deaf. Learning a language is great in helping a child understand training and learning something with lots of practice and perseverance.

You may want to memorize this week's memory verse in English and sign language.

If you are more interested in learning another language, you can do that as well. Our family loves learning other languages, and we practice Spanish and Mandarin regularly, and some of us also use American Sign Language now and then. You never know when it's going to come in handy! 😊

Picture Books: *Practice Makes Perfect* by Rosemary Wells, *The Girl Who Makes a Million Mistakes* by Brenda Li, *His Grace Is Enough* by Melissa Kruger

Build

For Mom and Dad
Preparing our Hearts

Scripture: Luke 6:46-49:1 Corinthians 3:9-15

Our younger daughter is going through a lot of changes in her life right now. She came back home after about a year of traveling around the world and started a new job, moved to a new area, and is jumping into adulting with both feet.

Our children have been raised in church since they were infants, and all have professed faith in Christ. We have tried hard to help them build a strong foundation for their faith. It seems in their 20's that that foundation is really put to the test. We've seen it with each of our children, but Annie is going through it right now.

Her new job is challenging but exciting, and she was offered a promotion after only being on the job for three weeks. However, she wasn't thrilled with some of the decisions the bosses have made and thought about turning down the promotion. Her boss talked with her and said, "Aren't you a Christian, a person of faith?" She said yes. He then asked her if she'd prayed about her decision to accept or reject the promotion. She admitted that her parents had been saying she needed to do that too, but she had not been praying about what God wanted her to do. She changed that immediately.

Sometimes, as the storms of life come at us, we see more clearly where our faith lies, what foundation we've built our faith upon. For my daughter, and for many of us, especially as Americans, we tend toward an attitude of trying to do everything ourselves, doing what seems best in our own eyes, and thinking we are smart enough and tough enough to navigate this life on our own, even though we also say we are Christ followers.

If our foundation is the Rock, Jesus Christ, then we will live like it. We will pray about where our lives are headed. We will pray about what God wants us to do. We will step out in faith and trust God. When we catch ourselves fretting or fearful, we know we've ignored the foundation of our faith and shifted to standing in the sand. We all do it at times, but we can step right back on the path and start building on the right foundation once again.

Prayer: We need to pray today that God will open our eyes when we've started building sandcastles instead of lives on the rock. Our world and our families need us to build on the strong foundation of faith and God's word. We can pray today for God's forgiveness, guidance, and wisdom as we let him build our lives in the strength of faith and obedience.

Preparing to Parent

We're fighting our culture here. As we teach our children, we need to be aware of the tug-of-war in their minds and hearts. We want them to have a strong work ethic. We want them to problem-solve and make decisions and then act on those decisions. We want them to be strong people who can stand up and be responsible adults. However, in our work to help them become those strong, responsible adults, we sometimes send the wrong message. The strongest and safest we ever are, is when we are in the center of God's will. That doesn't mean we are in a safe place by human standards, but we are spiritually safe, building on the rock.

God will help us. His word encourages us to be hard workers and to teach our children to be hard workers. However, he also wants our lives built on the right foundation of faith and his word. Hopefully this lesson will help clarify some of these ideas for our children, but we need to be aware of how they are processing all of this.

Matthew 6:33 comes to mind — we need to seek God's kingdom first, and then everything else will be added. This is the attitude and life we need to help our children recognize and adopt.

For the Family
Enjoying the Lesson Together

Scripture: Luke 6:46-49
(remember to choose a verse as your family memory verse with each lesson)

Object Lesson: Buildings and Foundations

This is an actual demonstration of what the story talks about. Each family member builds a house. You can do it 3 little pigs style if you want — one chooses the solid foundation while others build on the sand and maybe on something else unstable. You can build the houses and do the demo in the house if you don't mind the mess. I recommend going outside instead.

Supplies needed:
A big bucket of water and the ability to refill it.
Legos or other tools for building houses such as small boxes
Some sand
A big solid rock
Other possible poor foundations: flour, sugar, dirt, cotton balls (or let your family come up with some wild ideas to try)
Double stick super holding tape

Everyone builds a house, then water is poured over the house and foundation. The houses should fall or at least slide down. On the rock, the house might wash away, so find some way to fasten it to the rock first. Then, let the rains come, and, hopefully, the house stands. (If you have the double-stick super tape, that would be ideal to put under that house. To be fair, you could put it under each house, and they all should fall except the last one).

Read the scripture and talk about what we mean by building a strong foundation. We're talking about our faith and building it on what God says and being obedient to what he says. If we don't obey, our foundation isn't strong. If we obey something other than what God says, our foundation is wrong and is not strong.

Prayer/Song/Poem: Sing the old song we learned as kids about the wise man building his house on the rock. If you don't know it, you should be able to find it online.

Activity: Building from Bible Verses

See how big of a house your family can build out of Lego blocks using one block for each verse the family has memorized and can say out loud. It may be a verse one member knows and others the whole family can repeat together. Be sure to build it on a rock foundation. 😊

Picture Books: *Where Is Wisdom?* by Scott James, *Stories Jesus Told: The Story of the Two Builders* by Tim Ladwig or *The House that Went Splat* by Steph Williams, *Fly!* by Mark Teague; *The Spyglass* by Richard Paul Evans

Wait

For Mom and Dad
Preparing Our Hearts

Scripture: Isaiah 40:31

When I think of waiting, one time in my life stands out more than others. We returned home from the mission field after seven years on the field to help family and let our kids attend American school for a year. When we first arrived, finding work was hard. We knew we were most likely returning to the mission field at some point, but we didn't know when or how. My mom was ill, and Dave's dad had Alzheimer's, and our families needed our help. For months, we were simply in what felt like a holding pattern. A friend gave me a book to read about waiting on the Lord. It was the most painful book I've ever read. Every page emphasized my impatience and insecurities. It was a good book, but I was going through a hard time. The one wise thing we did during the time of waiting was keep working and serving. Whatever opportunities opened up, we helped. We waited. We prayed. We agonized. Eventually, we felt God's answers to our prayers, but those did not come quickly. The time with our families was precious. And waiting, as painful as it was, helped us draw closer to God and to one another in the waiting.

For most of us, learning to wait is difficult and almost painful at times. This is especially true when we are waiting on something we know is God's will, but we still must wait for the timing. This might happen when we're in college preparing for our future job or ministry, or while we're engaged and waiting for the wedding or maybe when we're pregnant waiting for the baby to be born. We'd rather just get on with living and want things to hurry along.

Part of what makes waiting hard is anticipation, but God is so merciful. During the waiting, we aren't just sitting idly by waiting for things to happen. We are working. We are getting ourselves and things ready. We're being obedient in what we know God has given us to do while waiting for the next part of our assignment.

What is God having you wait for today? What has he given you to do while you're waiting? Are there areas in your life where you need to be more faithful with what God has given you to do, where you've been too focused on the future instead of the present? Let God renew your strength and sense of purpose in today's responsibilities while you anticipate the next steps of his plan.

When I think of God renewing our strength as we wait, I remember that the joy of the Lord is our strength. He is working out his plan right now in our lives, even if that means waiting, grieving, or rebuilding, and as we wait, his joy strengthens and helps us walk through the difficult times.

Prayer: Today, let's pray for joy and strength. We always joke about not praying for patience because God will give us situations that require patience. However, if we are already in a waiting situation, we need patience and peace. I find praying for patience is a good prayer.

Preparing to Parent

In teaching today's lesson, we want to make sure not to frustrate our children to the point of discouragement or anger.

We also need to be aware of how we model patience and waiting. Think about what you say when waiting on hold on the phone. What about when following a slow driver in traffic? You may have other areas that push your impatience button, but those are two of mine.

Our goal is to help our children understand that waiting is part of life, part of God's plan, and is something to handle with grace and integrity.

Scripture: Psalm 27:14; Psalm 5:1-3; Psalm 40:1; Psalm 62:1-2, 5-8; Romans 15:4; Isaiah 40:31

(remember to choose a verse as your family memory verse with each lesson)

Object Lesson: Car trip

If possible, plan a longer car trip of at least a few hours.

If you have movies for the kids while you travel, assign an order in which videos will be chosen. Everyone must wait for their turn to choose.

Point out how we must wait our turn in restaurants or at the store or even when getting gas for the car. However, when we wait, in the end we are blessed with the movie we want to watch, our food, and gas for the car so we can go on our trip.

We even must wait while we drive to our destination.

If you can take a picnic lunch to a park or go to a dinosaur museum—whatever would be a fun outing for your family, but don't tell your children where you are going. God doesn't always let us know where we're going, but we trust him and know we will be blessed by his plan for our lives.

When you get to your destination, while eating lunch together, talk about waiting.

Ask questions like:
1. How does it feel when you have to wait your turn?
2. What happens when you are patient and wait your turn?
3. When we told you to wait for where we were going today, was it worth it?
4. Was it difficult to wait?
5. Did you trust that we had a fun surprise for you?
6. The Bible says we should wait on God, for him to show us his plan. How does that make you feel?
7. Can we trust God knowing that he has the best plan for us?

8. Why do you think God wants us to wait sometimes?
9. We want to learn to wait patiently. How can we wait patiently?
10. What can we do to keep a good attitude while waiting?

Prayer/Song/Poem:

Dear Lord, I pray
For patience today
For joy as I wait
When the answer seems late
I trust your plan for me
So I wait patiently
In Jesus' name, amen

Activity: Puzzle

For the ride home, make a copy of the puzzle page for each child old enough to do it and try to have some Bible stories for each child to read about Bible characters who had to wait such as King David, Abraham, Joseph (in Genesis), Noah, Simeon, and others. Or just talk about the stories and have them do the puzzle sheet.

Picture Books: *Waiting Isn't Easy* by Mo Willems, *Berenstain Bears: Patience Please* by Mike Berenstain, *The Very Impatient Caterpillar* by Ross Burach, Harriet Hurry-Up and the Oh-So-Slow-Day! By Allia Zobel Nolan

Who Had to Wait in the Bible?

```
Z B O Z M Y E Y E S E Q C E L
X O G P A Q M S E D I V A D W
Q C Q H H O F S G F C W Y P G
V A X A A W O T S Q B R U G D
S J V O R M E L I Z A B E T H
J A U W B W X H D L M Q S Z E
A H R C A J O T G V R R N J K
S A A A K F V J B N M I K A L
E A J N H B W Q S C D R E O Q
V G O I N C T I Y O T M D X Z
M Z S M J A M G L P K E N S J
A P E R Z E H P M H K T R P T
H S P W O J H Z T V A L O U R
Q A H N H I C U Y R N O B Z K
V P P I W J Z Z H P B C N V G
```

- Abraham
- David
- Elizabeth
- Hannah
- Jacob
- Joseph
- Moses
- Noah
- Sarah
- Simeon

How long did they wait?

_____ waited over 10 years to become king after he was anointed.

_____ waited 90 years before becoming the mother of Isaac.

_____ waited many years to see the baby Jesus. God told him he would see Jesus before he died.

_____ waited at least 75 years for the flood to come and more than a year for dry land to appear again after entering the ark.

_____ waited about 13 years to see his dream of becoming a ruler come true.

_____ waited 40 years in the desert before returning to Egypt to help free the Hebrew people and then wandered 40 years in the desert before dying right before they entered the Promised Land.

_____ waited 100 years before becoming the father of Isaac.

_____ waited many years before giving birth to Samuel.

_____ waited 14 years to marry Rachel and 20 years away from his brother Esau.

_____ was 88 years old when she became the mother of John the Baptist.

Humble

For Mom and Dad
Preparing our Hearts

Scripture: James 4:10; Luke 18:9-14; Philippians 2:3; Matthew 6:1-18; Romans 12:3

Early in our ministry, I went through a very odd time in my walk with God. God had given me the ability to discern some situations, and I even interpreted a dream for someone. The problem was, I had not been raised in a church where these things happened very often, and I didn't know how to handle these gifts properly. I found myself battling pride. Of course, we should never find the gifts of God a source of pride, but I was immature, and I did. It is one of my biggest embarrassments and regrets in my Christian Walk. I've dealt with pride in other situations, and I think we all battle pride because the very nature of sin is selfishness and self-focused choices. However, when it comes to pride in ministry, it is ugly and hurtful and evil.

When we seek experiences over relationship, the sensational over the deep things of God, we are in dangerous territory. Humbling ourselves before God is our only way to restoration. Reconciling and asking for forgiveness from those we hurt in the process is an uncomfortable but necessary step. Humility is a gift. When we are humble before God, we can hear him more clearly and follow him more faithfully.

Pride will hurt what God has been trying to do in and through our lives. Our goal is to glorify him which means to make his name known. When pride gets in the way, we make our name known, not his. We lose out on blessings and relationship opportunities. Humility allows us to let God shine in and through our lives. However, beware of false humility where we put on an air of humility but are really focusing on ourselves and how others see us. Any time we are focusing on ourselves, especially with concern for what others think, we are not operating in true humility.

Prayer: We must pray for awareness — that God will show us when pride is trying to take over. We need to pray that we can remain God-focused and humble. This life we live is all about him, not us. We need to pray for victory in this area of our lives each day.

Preparing to Parent

Our world teaches pride and self-esteem. God's way is the opposite.

When our world thinks of humility, it thinks of putting oneself down and demeaning oneself. God's way is the opposite.

As parents, our task is huge sometimes, especially when we are so different and set apart from the culture in which we live. We need to help our children understand big ideas that we struggle with in our own lives. Humility is a tough one for most children. We aren't to be prideful, but we also aren't to tear ourselves down. We really are hoping to think less of ourselves and focus more on God and others. True humility knows what we are gifted in and talented at doing. We own that without puffing up and thinking we are better than others as a person. It's often like walking on a tightrope, keeping our focus where it should be.

When I was a child, I was super shy. I would cut myself down with every thought in my mind. I felt like a failure all the time. My mom would get onto me about it. She encouraged me to recognize that I was a good student and a good friend. She told me to stop saying bad things about myself.

So, then I felt good about myself, and then she would get onto me for being conceited.

I was so confused. I didn't know what to do or think. I didn't know how to be "right." It was very hard.

We do this to our children without meaning to. When we tell them to think of others before themselves, some will think that they don't matter and feel guilty every time they want something or have a need.

So how do we do this? How do we help our children understand humility properly, the way God intends?

1. We keep the conversation open, and that means we talk about what we're seeing in our kids' lives, not just scold them, but really talk through their attitudes and struggles.
2. We recognize that this is a hard concept for everyone. Our children need to know they aren't alone in struggling to master humility. It's something we will work on the rest of our lives.
3. We explain that our goal is to have God on the throne of our lives, not ourselves. That doesn't mean we don't have needs or wants, but our focus is on God and what he wants in our lives.
4. By thinking of others and helping others, we show that we are working on a humble heart. That doesn't mean we feel guilty when we need help. Everyone needs help now and then. However, we try to be aware of other people's needs as well and try to meet their needs when we can.
5. We can feel good about accomplishments, and we can acknowledge our gifts and talents. They are facts, not bragging rights. We can be grateful for how God has created us, and give him the credit, not try to take it for ourselves.

Hopefully these steps will help us and our children be able to humble ourselves before God and serve others faithfully.

For the Family
Enjoying the Lesson Together

Scripture: 1 Peter 5:5-8; Ephesians 4:2; Romans 12:3
 (remember to choose a verse as your family memory verse with each lesson)

Object Lesson: Egg Protection

> Supplies:
> Eggs
> Bubble wrap
> Boxes
> Paper
> Balloons
> Packing peanuts
> Anything else you can think of to cushion an egg such as a pair of socks and cotton balls

Each family member will have an egg that they are trying to protect from harm when they are dropped from a certain height such as standing on a kitchen stepstool.

After each person creates their safe package, the eggs are dropped from an equal distance, and we check the results. Whose eggs survived?

After this game, talk about how some people are sensitive or may have needs, and we should try to think of others and care for them. Sometimes that means we are careful around them so that we don't offend them or hurt them with what we say or do. This is putting others needs before our own because we care about them and love them.

Read the verses, especially the Ephesians and Philippians verses. Ask, "How can we honor others?" "How can we care for them and meet their needs?" We must think about them and pay attention. If we are only thinking about ourselves, we will not notice how others are feeling or what needs they have because our thoughts are on ourselves. Of course, sometimes we have needs or need help. That's okay, but when we only think of ourselves, that is pride and selfishness. When we think of God and others, we are being humble.

Prayer/Song/Poem: Each child either writes a poem or draws a picture of what it means to be humble. This way we can confirm more easily how they understand what we're talking about.

Activity: Think About It

Read the different scenarios and ask if each person is being proud or humble.

1. Sarah walks to school with Sam each day. Sam realizes that Sarah is carrying some heavy books and could use some help. He offers to help her, but she refuses his help. She doesn't think she deserves to have help because it would be a bother to another person. (Sarah is being proud. When someone offers to help, and we refuse because we don't think we deserve it, we deny that person getting to bless us, and we are focusing on our faults and thinking badly about ourselves — we are thinking of ourselves which is not being humble).
2. Sarah and Sam are walking to school, and Sarah is carrying some heavy books. She even moans a little and complains that her arms hurt. She doesn't ask for help, but Sam doesn't take the hint. Sarah gets a little upset with Sam for not helping her, but she realizes she never really asked for help. (Both Sarah and Sam are being proud. Sarah is on the verge of humility because she realizes she was playing games instead of asking for help. Humility simply admits when we need help and asks for help.)
3. Sarah and Sam are walking to school, and Sam offers to help Sarah carry some of her heavy books. She thanks him and smiles a huge smile. She gives him a couple of her books to lighten her load, and they walk on to school together feeling happy. (An Ideal scenario. Both Sarah and Sam are being humble and are acting in ways that please God and bless each other.)
4. Sarah carries a bunch of heavy books to school. Sam offers to help her carry them, and Sarah gets upset. "What, just because I'm a girl, you think I can't carry heavy books? I'm strong. I don't need your help." (Sam is being humble, while Sarah is

being proud. Sarah seems to have a real issue with pride and defensiveness judging what she thinks Sam thinks even though she doesn't know what he actually thinks. Her pride is causing her to assume rather than communicate with Sam. This is probably the worst scenario)

How would you describe Sarah and Sam in each of these situations? Who is being humble? Who is being proud? How can they show true humility even better?

Picture Books: *The Tower* by Richard Paul Evans, *Not a Bragger* by Lee Ann Mancini, *Diva Delores* by Laura Sassi

Forgive

For Mom and Dad
Preparing our Hearts

Scripture: Matthew 6:14-15; Matthew 18:21-35

One Christmas, my uncle turned his life over to Christ. He and my aunt were profoundly changed as she recommitted her life to Christ, and he first believed. He told us what held him back for so long was the fact that he needed to forgive so many people. That Christmas, somehow God enabled him to forgive, and he then was able to open his heart to Christ, and he was never the same again. In fact, I never saw him even get angry at a person, much less hold a grudge. But he had it right. He understood that he could not be forgiven if he held unforgiveness in his heart.

We may struggle with this. It isn't easy. However, with God, all things are possible. He can enable us to forgive even the most terrible hurts, even over and over again.

Today, people try to make this all about ourselves — we forgive so we can be set free, and although that is certainly part of what happens when we forgive, a selfish forgiveness may not really be true forgiveness. When we forgive, we decide to let go of any anger, bitterness, or hurt we have toward the person.

It does not mean that we are saying what the person did was okay. When we sin, it is not okay. When anyone sins, it is not okay. Forgiveness never says sin is okay. If sin were okay, we wouldn't need a Savior. We wouldn't need forgiveness or to forgive.

So, if we are having trouble forgiving, we need to ask God to help us forgive. He will do it. And if we are trying to forgive by making excuses for someone or saying it was okay that a person hurt us, we are living a lie. We may wind up creating a sense of depression or trying to find a way to blame ourselves. This is also not dealing with the injury/sin and avoiding it. Jesus wants us to deal with it and let go of it. We are to leave the situation and the person in his hands, and he will deal with it in his wisdom and righteousness.

Forgiveness is one of those key elements of our walk with God that Satan tries to confuse and lie about. We must get this right for our sake and the other person's sake. The scriptures are clear.

The good news is that forgiveness sets us free whether we are receiving forgiveness or giving it. We put our trust completely in Christ to cover our sin and to deal with the other person's sin. That freedom is a blessing that draws us closer to Christ.

Of course, we are imperfect humans, and if we've been deeply hurt, sometimes we find we need to forgive again when our minds start replaying the anger and hurt. We need to ask God to forgive us for picking up the offense again, and we can ask him to help us truly forgive. The enemy likes nothing better than to keep us bound up in the sin of unforgiveness.

Prayer: If you are struggling to forgive, ask God. He will answer this prayer every time. Then, thank God for all his forgiveness he has lavished on you.

Preparing to Parent

Even though we must teach our children to forgive, we should not teach our children to express that forgiveness as "That's okay." Or "Never mind." They may feel uncomfortable saying, "I forgive you." However, that really is the only way to appropriately express forgiveness.

We want our children to understand God's amazing and generous and complete forgiveness. And we also want them to understand the importance of forgiving others. But we do not want to set them up to pretend what someone did was okay. We don't want them to turn their anger in on themselves. We don't want them to make excuses for their own sin or the sin of others. If forgiveness is needed, the offense and pain is real. The broken relationship is real. We must help them rebuild their relationships and rebuild trust.

We are teaching them how to handle relationships later in life as we teach them how to deal with small offenses as children.

For the Family
Enjoying the Lesson Together

Scripture: Matthew 6:14-15; Matthew 18:21-35
(remember to choose a verse as your family memory verse with each lesson)

Object Lesson: Dry Erase Board

Supplies needed:
Dry erase board
Dry erase markers
Eraser
Dry erase board cleanser

This is a very simple object lesson. Ask the children to tell something that someone might do to them that needs to be forgiven. Write these on the board.

Hopefully, when someone hurts our feelings or does something wrong to us, they'll ask us for forgiveness. When they do, we respond by saying, "I forgive you." But don't say it unless you mean it.

If they don't ask us to forgive them, what should we do? Do we still need to forgive them? (read the scriptures)

Then, when we forgive them, it is like erasing the board. We forgive them and let go of our anger and desire to get back at them for what they've done. However, sometimes we can still see the shadow of the sin like we can see a shadow of the word on the board, or we don't completely erase it, so we remember what the person did. We can get angry with them all over again when we remember what they did. Satan will remind us what they did so we can get angry again.

Whenever we find ourselves upset again, we need to pray and ask God to help us forgive again. We don't need to tell the other person because this is just between us and God. It is a matter of our heart and our need to forgive.

Then, answer any questions the children may have.

Prayer/Song/Poem: Pray asking God to show us any unforgiveness we have in our hearts. Ask him to help you forgive. Then, pray silently or together saying, "Lord, I forgive <u>name</u> for <u>what they did</u>."

Activity: Family Games

1. A meaningful activity that requires some planning is to get several helium balloons. Let each family member write or draw something they need to forgive on the balloon with markers. Then release the balloons and let them float away. It helps them understand releasing and letting go of hurts.

2. Play the game where each child takes turns dropping clothes pins into a jar behind a chair. Each child sits on their knees on the chair trying to drop clothes pins into the jar on the ground behind the chair. Most will miss the mark. Talk about how sin means we've missed the mark of God's righteousness and perfection. He forgives us completely when we turn away from our sin. That's why he tells us to forgive others. We have been forgiven for so much.

3. Play a Pictionary game with the white board. If you want to keep it on a spiritual note, have clues for Bible stories and see if your family can guess the story and retell the story.

Picture Books: *I Forgive You: Love We Can Hear, Ask For, and Give* by Nicole Lataif, *Forgive and Let Go!* By Cheri J. Meiners, *The Friend Who Forgives* by Dan DeWitt, *The Forgiving Tree* by Jan and Mike Berenstain, *The Lord's Prayer for All God's Children* by Harold L. Senkbeil, *Izzy's Notebook* by Terrie Hellard-Brown

Heap

For Mom and Dad
Preparing Our Hearts

Scripture: Proverbs 25:21-22; Romans 12:20

My husband is one of the most merciful people I know. He forgives and loves people who have treated him so badly. One couple did their best to make our ministry lives miserable at one of the churches where we worked. Dave continued to love them and serve with them. It took about six years, but then, the wife repented and began to support us. The husband never did change that we know of, but with his wife's influence, he wasn't quite as busy working against us. Heaping coals of fire or doing kindnesses to those who seek to harm us, is not easy for any of us, but with God, we can do it. The Holy Spirit will enable us, even those of us who aren't supernaturally gifted in showing mercy. It is worth it when people find their way back to a right relationship with God and hopefully a friendship with us.

God calls us as his children to live better than our cultures teach us or than our own selfish desires draw us. He calls us to let go of our rights sometimes and put others first for the sake of his kingdom and his purposes. One of those situations is when dealing with our enemies. The world says stand up for your own rights, sue whoever goes against you, and demand that people meet your needs.

We know this is not how God wants us to behave. Jesus turns the world's ideas upside down. "Love your enemies. Pray for those who persecute you. Turn the other cheek," Jesus tells us. We may not find it hard to pray for those who irritate us, but if they persecute us, we might have a harder time. No one enjoys being maltreated. Loving our enemies is not easy at all. We may hope they find some happiness or kindness but loving them means putting my forgiveness into action. It means I need to see them as Jesus sees them. It means I remember that our struggle here on earth is not against flesh and blood but against the evil powers we don't see (Ephesians 6:12).

One pastor told us that if we could sincerely pray for God to bless someone who had wronged us, we know we've truly forgiven them which means we've moved closer to loving that person. An article I read as a teen encouraged us to find an act of kindness that we could do for someone who has been an enemy. Our love needs feet; it needs action and less reaction.

Before we try to teach this lesson to our kids, we need to learn it for ourselves. We need to pray and ask God to show us where we may be harboring hard feelings and unforgiveness. We cannot love our enemies if we are not forgiving them.

Pray: We need to pray for God to reveal any unforgiveness and bitterness trying to take root in our hearts. We must pray for God to help us love others, even our enemies.

Preparing to Parent:
This lesson has an unusual analogy or image of "heaping coals of fire" on someone's head. Many have tried to understand this clearly, and some have said it resembles a practice in Ethiopia where a person carried coals on their heads as a sign of repentance and humility.

When I was a child, my teacher said how important keeping fires going was in the Middle Eastern cultures of Bible, and if a neighbor's fire went out, they would give coals to their neighbor who would carry the coals in a container on their heads back to their home. Kenneth Samuel Wuest (1893-1962) said, "In Bible times an oriental needed to keep his hearth fire going all the time in order to insure fire for cooking and warmth. If it went out, he had to go to a neighbour for some live coals of fire. These he would carry on his head in a container, oriental fashion, back to his home. The person who would give him some live coals would be meeting his desperate need and showing him an outstanding kindness. If he would heap the container with coals, the man would be sure of getting some home still burning. The one injured would be returning kindness for injury." (Quoted by *His Kingdom Prophecy*, "Do You Heap Burning Coals on Your Enemy's Head?" August 30, 2011.)

Scripture mentions in several places burning coals raining on a person as a symbol of Judgement such as in Psalm 116. So, the idea behind Paul's words is that in our kindness, coals of judgement for the person's wrongdoing falls upon them to convict them, and hopefully they repent.

However, we know we aren't literally to put coals of fire on someone else's head, and we can understand that our words or good deeds accomplish this when we show kindness in return for unkindness. When we bless others, we show that we know God, and it helps humble others and hopefully help them learn to follow God as well.

Of course, we are not responsible for other's reactions to our kindnesses. We are only responsible for our own hearts and attitudes. God is calling each of us to holiness and Christlikeness. Helping our children learn these important lessons is vital in their Christian growth. Being ready to answer their questions and really help them wrestle with their anger and unforgiveness may take more time than just a simple one-time lesson. We need to be prepared and also help them understand that they can talk about their true feelings and give them to God allowing him to help them change their attitudes toward others.

This lesson is not meant to make our children feel guilty and like failures. It is meant to show them clearly how our attitudes and actions are to be different from those of the world, and we can help them find ways to act according to God's ways. Letting them know that it isn't easy and that you struggle sometimes too may go a long way to helping them avoid focusing on failure and to keep going to God for help.

For the Family
Enjoying the Lesson Together

Scripture: Proverbs 25:21-22; Romans 12:20; Mathew 5:43-47
(remember to choose a verse as your family memory verse with each lesson)

Object Lesson: Coals

Make an old-fashioned campfire or barbecue with briquettes. You need coals to help children picture what the verses are talking about.

Our word for today is "heap." That's kind of a funny one, don't you think? What does the verb heap mean? How does the word heap apply to us when following Jesus? What do you think?

When we heap up the coals of the fire, what happens?

Do you think that these verses literally mean we should put hot burning coals on someone's head? That doesn't sound very nice or safe, does it? No, this is a symbol or analogy of what we do when we do kind things to those who are mean to us.

Jesus tells us to love our enemies and to bless them.

Read Matthew 5:43-47.

Heaping coals on someone's head means heaping kindness on them even when they are not kind to us. The hope is that the person will be humbled by our actions and become a friend, but sometimes, instead, they can get angry. We can't control how they respond, but we can control how we respond to them. We must make the choice now to act kindly towards others and show God's love to them. If we pray, God will help us show love even when someone hurts our feelings.

Activity: Role Playing (Practicing for Real Life)

The activity for today is role playing because loving our enemies can be easy to say but very hard to do. We need to practice, so we know how to respond when people are rude or hurt our feelings. So, give each child a different scenario to think about, and maybe have the whole family chime in with ideas of how to respond.

1. The class bully calls you a bad name.
2. You hear an adult complain about the children in church being too messy and too noisy.
3. You think your classmate stole your money. You don't have proof, but then he teases you about not having an offering that day.
4. Your cousin has always been your best friend, but this time when he visits, he will hardly talk to you.
5. Your sister takes the last cookie and laughs because you didn't get it.
6. You find out someone you thought was your friend said something mean about you to someone else.
7. You don't like your music teacher. She's just mean and unhappy all the time.

End with prayer asking God to help each of us react in a godlier way to those around us. If your children see negative things on the news or Internet, spend some time praying as a family for those who are angry and don't have love in their hearts for others.

A great song is on YouTube: "Love Your Enemies" by Kyle Sigmon

Picture Books: *Enemy Pie* by Derek Munson, *The Not Friendly Friend* by Christina Furnival (this book talks about boundaries, but it shows setting boundaries with kindness, calmness, and care), *Somebody Loves You, Mr. Hatch* by Eileen Spinelli

Keep (Your Word)

For Mom and Dad
Preparing our Hearts

Scripture: Matthew 5:33-37

I had a friend when I was little who almost always broke her word when she planned to come to my house. I would go to her house often, and she would plan to come to my house, but then at the last minute, she would cancel. Now, I recognize that she was just more comfortable at her house and would rather me come over there. Her house had a lot more to do than mine too. But as a child, I was so hurt and disappointed and wondered if she even really liked me.

Breaking our word has consequences far beyond just disappointing someone. We lose our integrity. People don't know if we are truthful and trustworthy. They don't know if we are lying when we tell them something. Our integrity is a precious possession we should guard at all costs. Trust is so hard to rebuild, and sometimes, with some people, it is impossible to rebuild.

The Bible even goes so far as to say that if we are trustworthy, people will know we are followers of God.

A simple answer from a person of integrity is enough. We don't have to add a pinky swear or any other kind of swearing to prove how serious we are. Our yes or no is enough. We need to be that kind of Christian.

Prayer: We need to be brutally honest with ourselves and ask God to search our hearts. We need to allow him to show us if we are being untrustworthy in any area of our lives, and if so, we need to repent. We can pray that God will help us be people of integrity in all we do and in everything we say.

Preparing to Parent

Sometimes it seems that nothing crushes a child's spirit faster than a broken promise. If we promise to take them somewhere, and we must change our plans, it seems to them that the world is ending. The disappointment is enough to crush our hearts. We've failed. We've let them down even if they don't show it.

Three points we need to remember when we make a promise to our children:
1. We must do whatever we can to fulfill that promise. Breaking it has consequences. They don't trust us if we break promises often. They might become angry and rebellious sometimes as a result. They may become unsure if they can trust God and others because of our example.
2. When we must break a promise because of illness or circumstances beyond our control, we must explain it and let them know that we are so sorry. We must ask for their forgiveness and assure them we wouldn't cancel or change plans if we didn't have to.
3. We may want to consider not making promises often, especially if there is a chance we may need to break that promise. Rather, we can say, we hope to do this or that, but we need to make sure we can before we promise it because we don't want to break our promises. We need to be careful and wise when making a promise.

For the Family
Enjoying the Lesson Together

Scripture: Matthew 5:33-37; Numbers 23:19
(remember to choose a verse as your family memory verse with each lesson)

Object Lesson: Game with Prizes

In this lesson you will play a game with your kids and promise that each time they win, they will get a prize of candy (this is a lie). Choose a game that is short and that your children can win easily such as Connect Four or Go Fish.

Bring the prize box to the table, but keep the lid closed.

Inside the prize box should be vegetables that your children dislike or herbs. Parsley, spinach, cauliflower, broccoli, radishes, canned green beans, canned beets—whatever you have that will make them turn up their noses especially when they expect candy.

Each time a child wins a round, open the box a little and peek inside to get just the right prize. When they balk at the canned green beans or whatever you give them, say, "Well, I have lots of prizes in here. We're starting with the healthier options, but there's candy in here somewhere. Just keep winning. We'll get there."

By about the 3rd or 4th round of wins, the kids are most likely going to be complaining quite a bit.

Ask them why they are so upset. Didn't they get a prize? Of course, they are going to say you lied about the prize. You promised candy.

Read the verses and talk about what happens when we break our word. If you play more games, do they think you will give them candy? They will most likely be unsure or totally not believe you. Point out that they've always believed you. Why are they not believing you now? Point out how quickly they stopped trusting you.

When we break our word or tell a lie, we break the trust people have in us. They will feel that they cannot trust you and won't believe what you say. It takes work to rebuild that trust.

Sometimes we can't help it. We tell the truth, but then circumstances cause us to have to change our plans and break our word. We aren't perfect, but we try very hard to keep our word always. In these instances, the best we can do is be honest, apologize, and show that we are people of integrity and trustworthiness. We did not intend to change plans or break our word.

Who always keeps his word, keeps his promises? That's right, God does. We can always, always trust his promises. He will always keep his word.

Prayer/Song/Poem: If you like Disney, *Sofia the First* has a cute song called "Keeping Promises No Matter What."
Lifeway has a song called "God Keeps His Promises" with country flare to it.
Lakewood Kids has one called "God Keeps His Promises" which is based on Number 23:19.

Activity: God's Promises

God's promises: spend time finding God's promises or see what promises each of you knows and make a poster of God's promises. (And, if you want, let them have some candy since they didn't get it earlier).

Picture Books: *Horton Hatches and Egg* by Dr. Seuss, *The Pandas Who Promised* by Rachel Bright, *Quinn's Promise Rock* by Christie Thomas

Fix

For Mom and Dad
Preparing our Hearts

Scripture: Philippians 4:8; Hebrews 12:2; Proverbs 4:25

We were in Korea, camping in the mountains. It was their version of a youth retreat; it was our version of roughing it. We were near a beautiful river surrounded by the most amazing mountains with their peaks shrouded in clouds. The scenery was breath-taking. As we looked up at those mountains, we could not help but praise God for the glory of his creation. Our eyes were focused on our surroundings, but our spiritual eyes were fixed on God and thanking him.

In the same area was an old mine with a suspension bridge. The mine shafts were closed up, but let off a breeze that felt like sitting in front of an air conditioner. After we got some bad sunburns, we sat by one to enjoy the coolness. After a while, we decided to cross the suspension bridge (don't ask me why). This was a thin bridge where we could hold onto both sides as we walked. My future brother-in-law Danny thought it would be fun to make the bridge swing back and forth when I was midway across. I did not think it was fun at all. But I learned to keep my eyes focused on the bridge, not the movement of the bridge, the huge drop if I fell, or the delight of Danny. I had to keep my eyes focused and my thoughts focused on praying for God's help instead of my growing desire to hurt Danny.

Both of these, and so many other events that happened that weekend reiterated today's scriptures to me. When times are difficult, different, challenging, and downright terrifying, we must keep our eyes fixed on Jesus and the path we need to walk by faith.

If we take our eyes off Jesus, we are like Peter when he walked on water. We start to fix our eyes on the storms around us, and we sink. We are overwhelmed by our circumstances. However, when our eyes are fixed on Jesus, the author and perfector of our faith, we find strength to carry on and follow him faithfully.

Prayer: What storms or challenges are you facing today? Pray about them and leave them at Jesus' feet. Pray that your eyes can be fixed on Jesus and not the troubles of life or even the mundane activities of the day.

Preparing to Parent

Distractions. That's what a lot of the electronic devices we have bring into our lives. This is an area that is so hard because we like our devices too. However, as we go through this lesson, we may find that God is dealing with us about these distractions and at least limiting the time we spend on them.

As we parent our children through this lesson, our goal can be to help them recognize their need to limit their time on devices and to focus more on family and on God. We used to give tickets for devices, so the children were limited to 20-minute intervals on their games or watching television because that's what each ticket gave them. We also silence and turn our phones upside down at the table. We all are tempted to look at them otherwise. Some families have one day or one weekend each month when they don't use any electronics. Our family hasn't done that yet, but I think it would be amazing once we got past the withdrawals!

We all may need to make this a matter of prayer and let the Holy Spirit guide us, depending on how dependent our family is on electronics, and, hopefully after limiting electronics, our children will decide on their own to let go of some of their screen time out of their own self-discipline rather than the subject continuing to be a struggle.

Of course, when our children are very young, we should control that time for them, but as they get older, and if they have some classes online, it becomes more and more challenging.

We need God's help and our whole family to cooperate in fixing our eyes on Jesus rather than on a screen.

For the Family

Enjoying the Lesson Together

Scripture: Philippians 4:8; Hebrews 12:2; Proverbs 4:25

(remember to choose a verse as your family memory verse with each lesson)

Object Lesson: Looking through a Telescope

To start, you may need to explain the verb for today. We usually think of "fix" meaning we have something wrong we are changing and making right. However, in these verses, the meaning is more to focus or affix our eyes on Jesus. It's like having a stare down in a sense.

For fun, you can have pairs of family members do a stare off with one another and see who blinks first.

If you don't have a telescope, you may be able to find one in your area at a tourist spot or a friend who has one. If you can't find one, then make a pretend one using a simple rolled up piece of paper or a cardboard tube from inside rolls of paper products. Or you can use a magnifying glass to talk about the same lesson. You could also make the same point with a microscope. The point is that wherever we fix our gaze, that is what we see and notice. That is what we learn about and what we know.

After focusing the lens or paper tube on different items, read the verses and talk about how what we focus on is what we think about and what we pay attention to. When we fix our eyes on Jesus, that means that we keep him at the center of our lives and all we do. His words and his Spirit direct where we go and how we behave. We think about our choices based on what we know about God and what he's said. We must know God's word, however, so we know what God says.

Prayer/Song/Poem: Normally if we are going to sing a song, we sing one that is upbeat and fun, but Twila Paris has a beautiful song called "Fix Your Eyes," and it might be a special time to listen to this song and let your children simply draw a picture while they listen to the words. You may want to give them a prompt to draw things they want to focus on about God. What do they want to fix their eyes on?

Another choice could be to sing the old children's song "Be Careful Little Eyes What You See" or other children's song with a similar message or the hymn "Turn Your Eyes Upon Jesus."

Activity: Star Gazing

If you've been able to look through a telescope, spend some more time star gazing and enjoy some roasted marshmallows outside together. Even if you don't have a telescope, spending the evening looking at the stars and roasting marshmallows is still a fun time.

Picture Books: *The Spyglass* by Richard Paul Evans, *Look* by Gabi Snyder, *The Flashlight* by Lizi Boyd

Choose

For Mom and Dad
Preparing our Hearts

Scripture: Ephesians 2:10; 2 Timothy 1:7; Joshua 24:15

In 2015 we were serving as missionaries in Taiwan. Our children were growing up, and we faced the need to return home to help them get settled into their lives. We decided we would return home after our younger daughter, Annie, graduated from high school which would have been in June 2016. However, she became anorexic during her junior year. It happened so fast.

She seemed healthy and was making good choices, and then around Thanksgiving, it was like a switch flipped. By March and April, we felt like we were in the battle of our lives trying to keep her alive. We decided to move home earlier than we had planned. We praise God that we did. Annie was able to regain her health and is now an active, outgoing, happy person who loves to cook and even has a certification in nutrition.

As we prayed, one thing kept going through our minds. We could not react and make decisions based on fear. We needed to discern what was the best choice for our daughter and for our family. The temptation to make choices based on fear was overwhelming at times. But we refused. We prayed and made decisions, to the best of our abilities, based on faith and what we felt God was leading us to do.

I tell you this story because we still pray this prayer today. We all make so many choices each day, and we must choose to make choices based on wisdom and discernment from God's leadership. Most of the time, our choices are simple, non-life-changing little choices like which flavor of coffee we want, which outfit we're going to wear, or whether to go to lunch with a friend or not. However, sometimes we get a sense in our spirit not to have that coffee, to wear a different outfit, or to definitely have that lunch with that friend. Later, we realize it was God letting us in on his plan. Maybe we needed that money we planned to spend on the coffee to give to a homeless person we encountered that day. Maybe our car broke down that day and we needed to have pants and sensible shoes on instead. And maybe that lunch that seemed frivolous and fun was actually a divine appointment to minister to our friend or the waiter who brought us our food.

That's what is so wonderful about prayer and relying on God's wisdom. He knows the future. He knows our needs before we even have them. If we will put our choices in his hands, and if we will train ourselves to respond to those leadings in our spirit, we can become more a part of God's work in the world around us.

Sometimes our choices become the tools God uses to help us join him in his work. When we make choices based on God's leadership, then we see Ephesians 2:10 lived out in real time. But we also know our God is merciful and knows us well. He knows when we're going to ignore his promptings in our spirit because we're in a hurry or thinking about too many items on our to-do list. Even in this, we don't live in fear because we know God can work all things out to bring about his plan. We don't need to fear or worry, but we do need to seek to make choices that are wise and change our choices according to the leading of his Spirit or his Word. Then, even when we don't understand we know that God is at work in and through our lives and in the choices we make.

Preparing to Parent

Do you remember the first month of being a parent? It seemed that every decision, every choice was life-shattering. I remember wondering if we'd chosen the right diapers, wipes, shampoo, EVERYTHING! It's kind of a miracle that we don't lose our minds in those early days of so many choices.

Just because we are more experienced now, that doesn't mean some decisions and choices about our children are easy. Choices about school, doctors, friends, church, even what's for dinner—all the choices we must make as parents will either make our faith and prayer life stronger or tempt us to be completely overwhelmed by life.

The way we make choices and handle tough decisions teaches our children a great deal about how to manage their own lives. We can teach them to be fearless because we serve the Almighty, All-Knowing God. Or we can teach them to fret and develop anxiety about life. We also can affect them by how we react to their choices. Do we condemn? Freak out? Or respond with grace and patience? (probably all of the above at different times).

If we can model godly decision-making, our children can grow up to be confident, God-trusting adults. We can plant those seeds with the daily choices and the big life choices we make each day.

For the Family
Enjoying the Lesson Together

Scripture: Proverbs 12:26; Proverbs 13:20; 1 Corinthians 15:33
(remember to choose a verse as your family memory verse with each lesson)

Object Lesson: Choosing Good Friends — Making a Grocery List

We make choices all the time. For instance, we choose what we want to eat for dinner. Let's do that now. What do want to eat for dinner tonight?

Once you decide, then start choosing what needs to be put on the grocery list.

For example: We want to make chili and cornbread. We have cornbread mix, but we need to buy milk and eggs.

What do we need for the chili?

As children name ingredients, you suggest some outrageous ones that don't go with the recipe.

Even though some items don't belong in the recipe, we still want them, like candy or super-hot chili peppers, but we may decide to make a wiser choice because our bodies will thank us later and they are better for us.

Finally, you have your list with the correct items on it.

Talk about how we find good friends. What "ingredients" make a good friend.

Let the children answer and you make a list.

Sometimes we may choose a friend because other people think that person is cool. How would God have us decide who makes a good friend? What is best for us and makes God happier?

What happens if we choose a friend who hits us or always insists that we do things we know we will get in trouble for?

What if we choose a friend who is unkind to others even though they seem nice to us?

We want to make good choices when it comes to shopping lists, but even better choices when it comes to friends.

Prayer/Song/Poem: Pray for your friends

Activity: Trip to the Grocery Store

Go to the grocery store together and talk about all the choices your family makes along the way — which seat to sit in, which way to drive to the store, where to park, which cart to choose, what to buy, etc.

When you get back home, while dinner is cooking, spend some time talking about how we make a lot of choices each day — what to wear, whether we will obey, what to eat — but some choices take more thought, and we can pray first before making those choices.

Here's a little prayer we can pray at those times (or you can make up your own.)

Dear Jesus, I have a choice. I want to choose what will make you happy because I know that will also be the best choice for me. I need your help. I need your wisdom. Help me choose right. In Jesus' name, amen.

Picture Books: *What If Everybody Did That?* by Ellen Javernick, *If Everybody Did* by Jo Ann Stover, *The Road Not Taken* by Robert Frost and illustrated by Vivian Mineker; *Will You Be Friends with Me?* by Kathleen Long Bostrom

Fan

For Mom and Dad
Preparing our Hearts

Scripture: Philippians 1:27

When we see people walking in their calling, we see such an amazing passion in their lives, and we sense the joy and rightness of the situation. I feel that way when I get up to teach. There is something divinely given to me when I teach. I can feel it. My husband and students comment on how they see it. My daughter has a heart for animals, and when she's caring for an animal, you see all her insecurities disappear. She is divinely gifted at working with animals, and they respond to her in such a beautiful way. In both of our situations, we have sought education to prepare better to use our gifts. We have welcomed opportunities as volunteers and employees to use our gifts. We work hard to fan into flame the gifting and passion God has given us.

Who are you? Specifically, who are you besides being a parent? Have you lost your focus, your identity, your purpose outside of being your child's parent?

It can happen. We carry a huge responsibility helping little humans grow into responsible adult individuals. And if we aren't careful, when they become those adults, we can find ourselves feeling we've lost our main purpose and direction in life.

This verse helps us keep perspective even while our little humans are still very little.

How many times have we heard about or seen marriages end when the kids go off to college or moms who can't seem to find their way wanting to continue to hold onto their kids while they are trying to become more independent. The turmoil and pain of these scenarios are not God's plan. As this verse from Philippians reminds us, we are citizens of heaven. We have a purpose and calling that far outweighs our role and calling as parents. In fact, in our role as parents, we are in partnership with God as He is drawing them to Himself.

Our true focus at the center of all we do in this life is our walk with God, growing more Christlike, and building up the kingdom of God. Our children are a part of that, but they are not the end all of that. We are working for eternal purposes, not just the eighteen or so years that we are busy parenting our children. Our marriage relationship, we hope, begins before we are parents and continues long afterward. Our walk with God should be at the center of all of the relationships in our lives and must go beyond them in its importance.

So today, as we think about fanning the flame of God's calling on our lives, let's focus on the calling outside of being parents. Who has God created you to be? What has God given you to do? Maybe, for a time, your only real ministry is your children, but we cannot let this wonderful gift rule out everything else God is doing in our lives and all that He wants to use our lives for long after our children are grown and on their own.

Prayer: Pray for the right focus and attitude. Pray for God to remind you who you are in Him beyond being a parent.

Preparing to Parent

One of the keys to this lesson is helping our children understand God's gifts and calling on their lives. Depending on their age and where they are in their walk with God, we may not have insight into anything beyond a calling for them to love God and love others. However, if you have a sense of gifts God has given your children, encourage them in those areas. Notice where they seem to be strong and help them learn to use those gifts wisely.

One of the odd things we have seen in today's Church is some congregations allowing very young children to lead in the services and minister to others during the service. They may prophesy, preach, or lay hands on people and pray. We want to encourage our children, but we also need to be wise. The Bible warns against putting someone too young in the Lord into leadership positions. They can be misled or misleading. Without maturity, they can become puffed up and get lost in their roles. We all need time to grow in our faith and understanding of God, and putting children into these positions too early can be harmful to them and to the Church. We must use wisdom and discernment.

So, yes, we want to encourage our children and help them feel at home in the Church. We want them to grow into their understanding that God has a plan for their lives. However, we don't want to put children into positions not meant for them. And we want them to first understand God's main purpose for them is a relationship with Him through Jesus Christ and for them to love God with all their hearts, minds, and souls and to love others before trying to navigate unsuitable things.

For the Family
Enjoying the Lesson Together

Scripture: 2 Timothy 1:6-7

Object Lesson: Build a fire.

Start a campfire, and watch it begin to smoke. Then, we fan it into flame. Roast hot dogs, marshmallows, or make s'mores for a fun family time. But make sure the children see you fan the fire into a flame.

Fan is a funny verb for us to talk about, but in Bible times it was common. They always kept hot coals ready to fan into a flame for cooking or for work. They didn't have stoves and gas or electricity like we do. They had to use fire.

Paul, talking to Timothy, said to his young friend to "fan into flame" the gifts God had given him. His faith was the number one gift. Then, God called Timothy to be a pastor, so that gift also needed to grow. God helps all of us grow and become who He created us to be. When you grow up, you may be a teacher, and God wants you to fan into flame that gift.

Paul tells Timothy that God has given us courage, power, love, and self-discipline. God also gives us these things. When we fan into flame the faith God has given us, we find courage instead of fear which allows us to love others, speak up with power, and to make good choices.

How can we fan into flame the faith God has given us?

Prayer/Song/Poem: Pray together for God to help each member of your family fan into flame the faith God has given you as well as fanning into the flame the other gifts and abilities He wants us to use.

Activity: Painting Fans

Either create fans folding paper back and forth or buy inexpensive Chinese paper fans. Either way, let children paint on each fan and write the Bible verses on each fan.

Picture Books: *The Tiny Seed, A Parable* by Katie Warner, *Little Pilgrim's Big Journey* by Tyler Van Halteren or *Little Pilgrim's Progress: The Illustrated Edition* by Helen L. Taylor

Respect

For Mom and Dad
Preparing our Hearts

Scripture: 1 Peter 2:17

When I was a young mom, I had a real problem dealing with traffic. My attitude was not good. I was impatient, and I often called other drivers idiots. I joked that my daughter's first word would be idiot. The truth is, I was feeling very convicted about my attitude toward those other drivers. I felt a little justified in my anger because I was driving trying to keep my child and myself safe in crazy California traffic, but the words I spoke, and my attitude was one of disrespect. I could try to rationalize it away, but the truth was I didn't respect others on the road like they were people. That was a place where God begin to work on me. God began to show me that I wasn't I truly loving others, and I certainly wasn't being respectful to them. Instead, I became hyper focused on myself and my own desires. It was a good lesson I desperately needed to learn.

The command in 1 Peter is a big one when we think of the way people treat each other. How will we respond to short-tempered, pushy people we may encounter? Deciding now how we will respond may help us when the time comes. But, more importantly, asking God to help us truly love people helps us find the respect and integrity we need when dealing with all people.

Respect grows into love and love helps create respect. These two really go together and build on each other, even in marriages. Love without respect can be fickle. Respect helps love become more stable and real.

As we prepare our hearts to teach our children, we really must ask God to examine our hearts. He needs to help us see our attitudes and be aware of the things we say. Do we perpetuate stereotypes? Do we get impatient and unkind toward someone in traffic or when waiting in line? Do we demonstrate respect for others, even our children?

Prayer: We should pray for God to reveal any attitudes we need to change, especially related to how we treat or think about others. We can ask God to help us love people, to really see people, and to care deeply about meeting the needs of others. We can also ask him to help us guide our children well in this lesson.

Preparing to Parent

If we show disrespect to others, our children will too. It's a quality they pick up on very quickly by our example. They take their cues from us on to treat others.

In addition, our children need to know that not only do we love them, but we also respect them. They pick up on our respect in simple, everyday encounters. For example, do we stop what we're doing and listen to their stories? Do we look them in the eye when talking to them? Do we encourage their dreams and ideas in genuine ways? Do we sometimes patronize them? Do we cut their stories short because we're busy? Do we only half listen because we're on our phones? Do we speak highly of them or complain about them to others? All these things build a clear understanding of respect or the lack of it to them. And they will copy what they see and experience.

So, as we prepare to parent, let's honestly evaluate ourselves and pray that God will help us improve and help our children to develop a true love and respect for others. We can ask God to help us model the right attitudes and actions toward others.

One final tip: if our child tends toward sarcasm or just lacks respect, we can sit them down and look them square in the eyes and talk heart-to-heart. We need to calmly explain that disrespect is ungodly and unacceptable. A child who has a quick wit and gets sarcasm often does not have the sophistication to know when they've gone too far-when they've gone beyond humor to hurting others and disrespecting them. Helping them find that place is vital, and if they can't master that, then we may caution them to keep their sarcasm to themselves so they don't hurt other's feelings and pray with them that they will learn to truly love and respect others. When this is done in a gentle and sincere way, they will usually respond well, especially if they are still young and not yet into their teenage angst.

For the Family
Enjoying the Lesson Together

Scripture: 1 Peter 2:17
(remember to choose a verse as your family memory verse with each lesson)

Object Lesson: Egg toss or water balloon toss

Supplies needed:
Water balloons or eggs (You may want to buy a water balloon filler. You can find them online).

Teams of two will toss eggs or water balloons trying not to break them. Each time they successfully toss the egg or balloon, they take a step back to make the distance between them wider for the next throw.

You may want to have a fun prize for the winners.

Afterwards, talk about how we sometimes have to be careful. If we had been tossing a rubber ball, we wouldn't worry about dropping it. It would be fine. It wouldn't break.

When we respect others, we bless them by caring for them. We know that some people are more sensitive and need to be treated more carefully than others. Respect for others helps us love them and care about their feelings and what they need.

Showing respect for others means we think about the other person and consider their feelings. We show respect and value them as a person. How do our words make them feel? What do our actions show them? How can we show more respect to our friends, to people we see in the community, and to our parents?

Prayer/Song/Poem: Really care in your heart and mind
Expect others to be kind
Say kind words with a good mood
Pray for God's help when others are rude
Express love and truly care
Consider your words before they're in the air
Think about other beings
Feel their many feelings
Use your heart to understand
Love and respect go hand in hand

Can you make your own acrostic poem for respect?

Activity: "Mother May I"

It's an old game, but it always reminds children to speak respectfully to their parents.

Picture Books: *Berenstain Bears: Show Some Respect* by Mike and Jan Berenstain, *Grumpy Monkey* by Suzanne Lang, *The Invisible Boy* by Trudy Ludwig, *The Little Respectful Spot* by Diane Alber

Encourage

For Mom and Dad
Preparing our Hearts

Scripture: Romans 1:8-12; Romans 15:4; 1 Thessalonians 5:11; Hebrews 10:24; Jude 1:3

We were at my dad's house. My dad is an army guy, and so encouragement is not something one hears from him very often. He's much more stoic. That day he said, "I don't understand..." I'll be honest, my first thought was that we'd done something stupid that he was going to comment on. But then he said, "I don't understand how you've lived by faith. I don't think I could have done what you have done all these years in Taiwan." I nearly burst into tears. His words meant so much to us. They affirmed us and the work God called us to. They encouraged us that we had made the right choice to follow God, and not only had God used us there, but he was using us here through the testimony of his work in our lives. My husband and I sometimes question what we've done. When my mom died, I especially questioned whether it was worth it to leave family and move overseas for so long. But my dad's words that day will always encourage me.

Dear parent,
This lesson is about encouraging one another, and I want to start by encouraging you today. Just as Paul said in Romans 1, your faith encourages me, and I hope my faith encourages you. As a parent who wants to grow in your faith and wants to lead your children to follow Christ, you are accepting the calling God has given each of us when we become parents. I'm so proud of you for taking your calling seriously. You are a blessing to your children, to the church, and to the future.

Our task is daunting, but God is with us through every decision and conversation. He has also given us the gifts we need to raise our children. He gives us his wisdom and guidance each day. In addition, he's given us our church families and friends to help us along the way. We don't walk this road alone.

We hear it said again and again today: "You've got this!" But it is true when God's got us in his hands, then we're able to be the best parent for the job of raising our amazing children. You are blessed, enabled, capable, and exactly what your children need — not in your own strength and abilities alone, but in God's. Praise the Lord today that we are not alone and pray that He will empower you to bless your children wisely. Be encouraged and strengthened.

Prayer: Today, let's pray for Christian parents who are working hard to make a difference in their children's lives and that we will influence the world in a positive way. As always, we should pray for wisdom as we continue to teach and guide our children and as we work out our own faith as disciples of Christ. God bless you and your family.

Preparing to Parent

You may have heard of the popular book by Gary Chapman called *The Five Love Languages.* One of those love languages is affirmations. As parents, we should consider what love language speaks to each child the most; however, I've never met a child who did not beam when they are affirmed or encouraged. It builds them up and helps them see that their lives matter.

When talking about encouragement and affirming someone, we aren't talking about flattery or simply talking about how the person looks. The Bible makes it clear that we are to build each other up and spur one another on to do good works. Our encouragement of our children should help them see who God has created them to be and what he has gifted them to do.

This week as we work through this lesson, we should look for ways to encourage our children in genuine, meaningful ways. We should pray that God opens our eyes to see each child as he does.

For the Family
Enjoying the Lesson Together

Scripture: 1 Thessalonians 5:11; Romans 15:4; Hebrews 10:24
(remember to choose a verse as your family memory verse with each lesson)

Object Lesson: Inflating a Ball

Supplies needed:
Flat ball
Air pump

Explain that the ball is flat and can't bounce. It only lies there not fulfilling what it was created for. But when we pump it up, suddenly it bounces and can be used to play all kinds of games.

People are like this ball. When we are discouraged and feeling sad, we are flat and feel useless. But when we are pumped up by the encouragement of others, we find that we are excited to do the things God created us to do. We are filled with joy.

When we encourage others, we help them bounce with joy. We help fill them with love and hope. Encouragement is powerful and can change everything just like the air in this ball changed everything for the ball.

Prayer/Song/Poem: We can pray to be encouragers. We can pray that we will notice when someone needs to be encouraged, and that we will notice how we can encourage people daily.

Activity: Board Games

Play some games together as a family. Encourage each other as you play. Cheer each other on. Then, enjoy some cold water together and talk about what they learned and how they feel.

Picture Books: *The World Needs Who You Were Made to Be* by Joanna Gaines, *Ordinary Mary's Positively Extraordinary Day* by Emily Pearson; *The Wonderful Things You Will Be* by Emily Winfield Martin; *Wherever You Go, I Want You to Know* by Melissa Kruger

Celebrate

For Mom and Dad
Preparing our Hearts

Scripture: Luke 15:11-32

One of my dolls, when I was a child, came in a box that looked like a suitcase. One day, I filled that box with clothes and planned to run away. I don't remember why, but I was determined. My mom saw my packed box in the living room and asked what I was doing. I told her I was running away. I expected her to get angry or upset, but all I remember was that she responded calmly. Within a few minutes of our talk, I was unpacking my box and staying home. I honestly can't remember what my mom said, but I do remember the feeling I had. I was part of a family. Running away was a bad choice. Staying, even though I was angry, was a better choice.

Unfortunately, in these scriptures we see a young man who did not choose to stay. He doesn't seem angry, just selfish and full of himself. He reflects the way we are when we ignore and reject God's gift of salvation. We walk away and try to live life on our own thinking we know what is best.

This story can apply to someone who is lost and needs to come to our Father in repentance, but the story seems even more applicable to those who know Jesus and have walked away. The older brother represents the faithful who have stayed faithful and how they often do not rejoice when someone comes back to Christ after rebelling. However, the point of either interpretation is the joy of the father when the son returns.

If we think of this when we're far from God, when we know we've made wrong choices, and the enemy is trying to tell us we've gone too far, that God can never forgive us or use our lives again, this story not only gives us hope, but should fill our lives with joy and peace as well. Our Father is waiting for us. He wants us to return. He wants to receive us and forgive us, restoring us to our place of sonship. We don't deserve any of it. Yet he lavishes his love and forgiveness on us.

Prayer: If you've wandered from God, recognize your need to return to the Father. Seek him and repent today. Return and celebrate God's great love and mercy. Let him embrace you in his arms and welcome you home. If you know others who have walked away from God and seem to have lost their way, pray for them today.

Preparing to Parent

How do we respond to a rebellious child? When they are young, we must intervene and discipline the child. We need to guide them and help them understand how dangerous a rebellious heart is. Obedience and respect for elders is imperative. This attitude often later translates into their spiritual life and their obedience and respect for Christ.

When they are older, we, like the father in the story, must pray, wait, and watch. We need to guard our hearts so that we do not allow bitterness to take over. We need to be ready with grace, mercy, and forgiveness.

Whatever stage of parenting we are in, we need to be praying for our children daily that their hearts will be softened toward God in every way. We can work toward keeping the conversation open with them even when they are in the midst of rebellion against God. It isn't easy. Pray for God's help and ask others to pray with you.

For the Family
Enjoying the Lesson Together

Scripture: Luke 15:10-32
   (remember to choose a verse as your family memory verse with each lesson)
Object Lesson: Share the Secret

For this lesson, you need to decide on something exciting to do like hiding a "treasure" your kids will love, and you only let one child know where it is and what it is. It's a secret, but at the right time, they get to share about it with their siblings. If you only have one child, then the child can share the secret with another family member (for example, Dad tells the secret, the child shares with Mom or Grandma).

If you have time to prepare, you could make a treasure hunt map, and even though the child knows what's in the treasure, they get to follow the map together to find it.

Whatever you decide, your child needs to be excited to share the secret.

For explanation purposes, I'm going to pretend you've hidden a box with a gift card for a dinner out at your favorite restaurant and a movie, and you've made a treasure map to follow.

Start by getting your child excited about it. Show him the box and what you're putting in it. Let him know that you plan to take the family out for a movie and dinner tonight after everyone finds the treasure. The prize is a secret for now while you hide the box, but after that, he gets to tell everyone they get to go on a treasure hunt together.

Once the box is hidden and the map is ready, call the family together and let the child share the secret that there is a treasure that he knows about, and he's going to help them find it. He shows them the map, and the hunt is on.

Once they find the box, meet back together and open it. Then, celebrate!

The lesson: The child knew a fun secret and shared it happily with the family. When we know Jesus, we have a treasure that we can share happily with others too. We celebrate what God has done in our lives and share that with others. When we celebrate what God is doing in our lives, everyone can celebrate and be happy.

In the story, the father celebrated that his son had returned. The story is about someone becoming a believer and follower of Christ. When we see someone decide to follow Jesus, we should always celebrate. Did you know that even the angels celebrate in heaven when someone decides to follow Jesus? They do. Read about it in Luke 15:10. And we should celebrate Jesus and what he's done in our lives every day too. God is so good!

Prayer/Song/Poem: Sing "Celebrate, Jesus, Celebrate!" or Paul Baloche's songs: "I Will Celebrate" or "Celebrate the Lord of Love"

Activity: Enjoying the Treasure

Of course, your activity is to go to the movies and eat dinner at your family's favorite restaurant. If you opt for a different treasure, then maybe you put the supplies for making s'mores in the box and spend the evening around the fire pit eating s'mores and chasing fireflies. Whatever you do, make it a meaningful celebration of your family.

Picture Books: *The Awesome Super Fantastic Forever Party* by Joni Eareckson Tada, *Don't Forget to Remember* by Ellie Holcomb, *Thank You, God* by J. Bradley Wigger

Serve

For Mom and Dad
Preparing our Hearts

Scripture: John 13:1-17; Matthew 20:28; Romans 12:11; Colossians 3:23; Matthew 25:31-46

I was serving at a youth camp one summer where we had some groups of girls who were so rude to each other. I prayed about what could be done, and the Lord opened my eyes to how long some of the girls' hair was, and I felt led to ask if I could braid their hair. I love doing French braids, and it gave me an opportunity to talk with them. The girls gathered around as I braided, and soon, the girls from the other group also came around and asked if I could braid their hair. In the next half hour or so of braiding hair, these girls began to talk to one another, and soon they are acting like friends instead of enemies. It wasn't exactly washing feet, but it always amazes me how God uses simple acts of kindness to change hearts.

I love how God uses ordinary people in ordinary ways to bless people extraordinarily. Only he can do that, and it's wonderful. When we think of serving others, we only need to ask God to open our eyes to the needs around us. He will show us areas where we can pray and where we can meet those needs. Even the smallest acts of service glorify God and make a difference in people's lives. We don't have to strive and fret and try so hard to make a difference in the world. It's most often the simple acts the Holy Spirit prompts us to do that makes someone's day or changes someone's life.

God uses our talents, interests, and gifts to bless others. We need to remember what Matthew 25 tells us: when we bless others, we are blessing God, and we demonstrate that we know and love God as we love others.

Prayer: What is God prompting you to do for someone today?

Preparing to Parent

As parents, one of the difficult truths to have our children embrace, at least some of our children, is the fact that we were created for work. Some children have the idea that they are to be served, not to serve. They don't like work, and they want to just have fun all day with no responsibility.

It doesn't help the situation that when they don't do their work, we punish them and get onto them, so they have an even more negative attitude about work.

We must start young by allowing kids to help with chores. It will build a sense of accomplishment and make them feel more a part of the family as they help. They feel important. And it sets the stage for a life of service and taking pride in work that is well-done.

We should work together. Showing children how to do chores well must be modeled. Some children really can't see all the clutter we want them to clean up in their room. Some are clueless as to how to successfully complete a chore. If we work together and model it carefully, we are discipling them well, and we are setting them up for success.

We must praise a job well-done. We need to show appreciation for their hard work and when they've successfully completed a job. If they struggle doing the job well, we should determine why and help them learn if necessary. Our goal is to help them build a good work ethic and sense of pride in what they do.

One note here: we need to be careful that we aren't expecting too much from them. Consider their age and ability before giving feedback. Sometimes we may feel it is just easier to do the job ourselves, and then it will be done to the level we want it done. It's difficult, but we need to resist that temptation. It will tear down all the good work we've accomplished, and it can discourage the child.

For the Family
Enjoying the Lesson Together

Scripture: Matthew 20:28; Romans 12:11; Colossians 3:23; Matthew 25:31-46; Psalm 100:2
(remember to choose a verse as your family memory verse with each lesson)

Object Lesson: Serving Scavenger Hunt

Everyone meets at the kitchen table to get instructions.

Each person has five minutes to find three things that we use to serve others. Think about things that can help you show God's love, help someone, or to be kind to someone else. Ready, set, go!

When everyone returns, have them share what they found. Talk about how we could use each item to serve others.

How does God usually bless people? By having others meet their needs or bless them in some way.

Read Matthew 25:31-46

Serving means that we do something for someone. It means work, sometimes hard work. Does work honor God? Let's look at the scriptures. Read the other verses.

How do you feel when you help someone?

How do you feel when you've done a good job?

Answer any questions and talk about how work is a blessing to us and helps us find our purpose and calling in life. Work pleases God and shows others that we know and love God.

Prayer/Song/Poem: Pray for God to show each family member how to serve someone this week.

Activity: Acts of Kindness

Who has served you lately? Write a thank you note and tell them how much they blessed you.

Get a calendar and make a list of some simple acts of kindness your family can do together in the next month. If you need help, here are a few ideas:

1. Collect your change all month and donate it to a food pantry or your church's missions fund.
2. Record a story on video to share with a family member: kids read a story to their grandparents
3. Donate gently used items to a local crisis nursery and include some essential new items such as packs of diapers or canned goods.
4. Write a letter to your pastor and his family thanking them for the ministry they do.
5. Leave a note on the mirror for someone in your family encouraging them with why you appreciate them and adding a Bible verse to inspire them.
6. Invite some friends over for an outdoor movie night. Project the movie onto your garage door.
7. Pay for a meal at your local restaurant in advance for someone in need.
8. Do a chore for one of your family members without them asking. Wash the dishes when it isn't your turn or surprise your mom by doing a chore she usually does. Wake up early and clean your room, surprising your mom and dad when they come to wake you up.
9. Read a bedtime story to your mom and dad.
10. After dinner, clear your dishes and your parents' dishes off the table. If you're old enough, rinse them and put them in the dishwasher.
11. Bring in your neighbor's garbage cans from the curb.

12. Go on a dust bunny hunt. Surprise your mom and dad by cleaning the dust bunnies under beds and in corners.

Picture Books: *The Little Red Hen* by J. P. Miller, *Be Kind* by Pat Zietlow Miller, *The Good Samaritan* by Ella K. Lindvall; *A Servant Like Jesus* by Lee Ann Mancini; *Ordinary Mary and Her Extraordinary Deed* by Emily Pearson; *The Invisible Boy* by Trudy Ludwig

Stand

For Mom and Dad
Preparing our Hearts

Scripture: Luke 21:5-38

When we lived in Taiwan, we went through a time when my husband Dave received death threats daily. The caller was using a burner phone, so the police couldn't find the person. He hated what Dave stood for and preached about. We lived next door to the church. Everyone knew where our apartment was, so we lived knowing that this person could get to our family just about any time he wanted. We prayed. We were as careful as we could be, but we had no intention of stopping the ministry or sharing the Gospel.

Before long, the police found the young man, and Dave was called to the police station. He was a confused young man who had lost his way. His mother was there with him at the station, and he was in serious trouble from her even though he was in his 20's. Dave chose not to press charges as long as he quit threatening him and didn't text him anymore. Even though this turned out well, and no one was hurt other than by some Chinese mother discipline, we had to make a choice in the midst of the situation — would we stand or hide?

As the times move closer to the end times, we will face trials that may involve being arrested, tortured, or killed. Some of our brothers and sisters face this today. And throughout history, we have had areas in the world that treated Christians and Jews horribly. It is normal in our world, and Jesus warned us about it. But he also encouraged us to stand strong and not to be afraid.

We know that God created us for the times in which we live. We know that God overcomes the world. We pray for help, for strength, for safety, and for faith. God will either deliver us or walk with us through the challenges of our age and culture. Stand firm, stand tall. Honor God with your life, even if your life is required of you.

Prayer: God knows we struggle sometimes with feeling overwhelmed or fearful. We can pray for his help and strength to carry us through whatever trials we may face. His grace is enough. We can hold onto it.

Preparing to Parent

During times of persecution, we must decide as parents how much to share with our children. We used to observe IDOP (The International Day of Prayer for the Persecuted). Our children were aware that some Christians today are persecuted for their faith. We prayed for them as a family and as a church. We used to sing a song called "Teach Your Children" by Jerry Chrisman with lyrics that said:

> Teach your children how to stand
> For there's an enemy in the land
> Lead them, Lord, by your right hand
> Teach your children how to stand
>
> Teach your children how to pray
> And drive the enemy away
> To hear your spirit and obey
> Teach your children how to pray
>
> Teach your children how to die
> Take up the cross, the world deny
> That Jesus may be glorified
> Teach your children how to die

It was a hard song to sing, but it has an important message for us. We need to, age appropriately, prepare our children to stand. Since we live in a country where we have had freedom of religion, we need to help our children understand that the world may not always let us have this freedom. We should be thankful for it now, but we should also be ready to stand when times get tough.

In countries where persecution is expected and is a way of life for believers, a person weighs the cost required when becoming a follower of Christ. It's not something they need to tell their children. One father, when asked why he didn't tell his children about persecution, he responded, "I don't tell my children the sun will rise each morning. It is a part of life, and we know it is going to happen." (a paraphrase from the movie *The Insanity of God*).

You may want to watch a couple movies to help understand the worldwide situation of persecution for yourself: *The Insanity of God* and *Sheep Among Wolves Volume 2* (on YouTube). These are for adults, not for little children.

What strikes me most in both movies is simply a shift in understanding and mindset. Those who live with persecution have a different mindset than those of us living in freedom.

Again, you will want to share what is age appropriate. Most of us in the USA will face more teasing or mocking than actual persecution, but that may change as Christ's return draws nearer, so helping our children learn how to respond to teasing and mocking with grace and love would be where we should start.

For the Family
Enjoying the Lesson Together

Scripture: Luke 21:28; 2 Corinthians 4:8-9
    (remember to choose a verse as your family memory verse with each lesson)

Object Lesson: Balance Games

>Supplies needed:
>Balloons
>Painters tape (if doing this indoors)
>Pool noodles
>Ropes

1. Play tug-of-war standing or on knees — if weight difference/age difference is an issue, have the younger/smaller child stand while the older/larger child or parent is on his/her knees.
2. Balance Beam — use a curb, painters tape line, or a long piece of wood about 4 inches wide and 5-6 feet long. Let each person practice walking on the balance beam, first in a normal way, then heel to toe. See how far they can go before falling off the line.
3. Balloon Volley — if you don't have pool noodles, just use your hands, or play twice using hands once and pool noodles second. The idea is to keep the balloon in the air. If you do individual volleys, each person can record their time of how long they kept the balloon aloft. If doing it as a family, see how long the family can keep the balloon in the air, but no one person wins or loses.
4. Freeze Frame — this one is really fun with little kids. It's like musical chairs except that everyone is just dancing while the music plays, and then when it stops, they must freeze and not move. If they move or fall, they are still in, but they just try again to not fall next time. The idea is to improve balance and remain standing.

After playing all these games, read the verses and talk about how sometimes people tease us about our faith, and Jesus tells us to stand up tall and don't be afraid. We can respond with determination but also with grace and love for others. When we get knocked down, we get back up again. Just like when we fell off the balance beam, we got back on and tried again. When we fell down in the tug-of-war, we didn't just lie on the ground forever. We got up and got ready for the next game. Whatever we are doing in life, when we fall down or get knocked down or frustrated, we get up and keep going. It is the same with our faith and trust in Jesus. Sometimes we mess up and make mistakes, but we don't stay there, we try again and keep going.

We are strong, and we can stand even when times are tough.

Prayer/Song/Poem: Pray together for faith and strength. Pray that we can be kind when others are unkind and loving when others are unloving.

Activity: Obstacle Course

If you want to do more, create an obstacle course to challenge your balance and skill. The family can build it together and then run through it a few times seeing if each person can beat their own time and then who is able to do the best.

Picture Books: *I'm Not Scared; You're Scared* by Seth Meyers, *The Girl Who Never Made Mistakes* by Mark Pett and Gary Rubinstein, *The Frightening Philippi Jail* by Gary Bower

Expect

For Mom and Dad
Preparing our Hearts

Scripture: Matthew 24:36; Luke 12:35-40; Revelation 22:20; 2 Peter 3:3-15a

When I was younger, I remember people praying the prayer in Revelation 22:20 asking for Jesus to return quickly. I didn't want Jesus to return quickly. I had an evangelist's heart. I was happy God was waiting. I would pray, God, help more people come to you first. It broke my heart to think of those who rejected Jesus.

We know God doesn't want anyone to die without knowing him. Even though we should live in expectancy of Jesus' return, and as the times become more and more difficult, we may pray boldly, "Lord, Jesus, come." But in the meantime, we should strive to see as many come to Jesus as possible. The best way for that to happen is through sharing our faith and discipling others who will share their faith and disciple others.

Are we ready? Are we working for the Kingdom of God? Are we discipling those who are younger in their faith?

We have so much to do, especially as we sense the time is drawing near for Christ's return.

Prayer: Today, we can pray for those we know who are far from God. We can pray that we are ready for Christ's return. We can pray that we remain strong and faithful as the time draws closer.

Preparing to Parent

The idea of Jesus' return can be frightening for children. When they hear sermons about it or read verses about it, the ideas can seem scary. We need to answer their questions, and we can help them understand what it means that Jesus is coming back, and to be ready. We need to keep our hearts right with God and help others know about Jesus. Honestly, that is really all we need to be focusing on as believers. Worrying about the times, the signs, and how it is all going to happen is not nearly as important as the Gospel and living out our faith.

The world is going to do what it is going to do. If we focus on the difficulties and the fear of those hard times, our kids could also begin carrying those burdens. However, if we focus on joy even in hard times, truth even when media is sensationalizing events, and hope during the fear and negativity of our age, we can help our children celebrate Jesus' return and learn to live their faith daily.

For the Family
Enjoying the Lesson Together

Scripture: Matthew 25:1-13
   (remember to choose a verse as your family memory verse with each lesson)

Object Lesson: Getting Ready

   Supplies needed:
   2 Bag of clothes (each with a complete outfit.)
   2 sets of items needed for a party: a present, the invitation, a party hat, a noise maker

   Two people will compete at a time.

Each will put on a complete outfit from their bag of clothes including shoes and accessories (tiara or party hat, gloves, jewelry — they must put on everything in their bag)

Then, they pick up the gift, invitation, and noise maker and shout, "I'm ready!"

Afterwards, read the scripture and explain the parable of the ten bridesmaids.

Jesus is coming back. It could be any time. When he returns, all things will be made new. We will have no more sadness, only joy, if we are ready. How can we be ready? Like the bridesmaids who were ready when the bridegroom came, we can be ready for Jesus. We first make sure we know Jesus as our Lord and Savior. We have chosen to follow him all our lives. Next, we try our best to tell others about him and help them be ready too. We can't be perfect. We will sin, but when we mess up, we pray and ask God to forgive us, and he does. We are close to him again.

If Jesus is our Lord and Savior, we don't need to be afraid or worry about when Jesus will return because we are ready.

Prayer/Song/Poem: "Even So Come" by Chris Tomlin is a beautiful song about Christ's return.

Activity: Family Celebration

If you can, plan for grandparents or family friends to come over and share a feast together. Have a guest bring balloons to add to the feeling of celebration.

You can surprise the children to emphasize how Jesus' return is unknown, and we just need to be ready.

Picture Books: *Jesus and His White Horse* by Jake McCandless, *Jesus and the Very Big Surprise* by Randall Goodgame, *Jesus Is Coming Back* by Debby Anderson

Index

Be sure to teach them to your children.
Talk about these commands when you sit in your house
and when you walk on the road.
Talk about them when you lie down and when you get up.
(Deuteronomy 6:7, ERV)

When You Sit in Your House
    At the Table
        16, 47, 67, 73, 78, 103, 118, 133, 161, 260
    Anywhere at Home
        21, 27, 44, 83, 87, 92, 109, 127, 151, 156, 176, 181, 193, 215, 221, 231, 256, 270
    In the Bathtub
        37
    Crafting at Home
        73, 87, 92, 98, 113, 138, 151, 244

When You Walk on the Road
    In the Car
        83, 210, 239
    In Nature
        31, 98, 113, 123, 138, 167, 172, 189, 198, 202, 206, 226, 235, 244, 248, 252, 265
    In the Rain
        186

When You Lie Down and When You Get Up
    At Bedtime
        60, 145
    In the Morning
        55

Made in the USA
Columbia, SC
23 February 2025